T0247776

Aristophanes: *Lysistrata*

BLOOMSBURY ANCIENT COMEDY COMPANIONS

Series editors: C. W. Marshall & Niall W. Slater

The Bloomsbury Ancient Comedy Companions present accessible introductions to the surviving comedies from Greece and Rome. Each volume provides an overview of the play's themes and situates it in its historical and literary contexts, recognizing that each play was intended in the first instance for performance. Volumes will be helpful for students and scholars, providing an overview of previous scholarship and offering new interpretations of ancient comedy.

Aristophanes: Frogs, C. W. Marshall
Aristophanes: Peace, Ian C. Storey
Menander: Epitrepontes, Alan H. Sommerstein
Menander: Samia, Matthew Wright
Plautus: Casina, David Christenson
Plautus: Curculio, T. H. M. Gellar-Goad
Plautus: Menaechmi, V. Sophie Klein
Plautus: Mostellaria, George Fredric Franko
Terence: Andria, Sander M. Goldberg

Aristophanes: *Lysistrata*

James Robson

BLOOMSBURY ACADEMIC
LONDON • NEW YORK • OXFORD • NEW DELHI • SYDNEY

BLOOMSBURY ACADEMIC
Bloomsbury Publishing Plc
50 Bedford Square, London, WC1B 3DP, UK
1385 Broadway, New York, NY 10018, USA
29 Earlsfort Terrace, Dublin 2, Ireland

BLOOMSBURY, BLOOMSBURY ACADEMIC and the Diana logo are
trademarks of Bloomsbury Publishing Plc

First published in Great Britain 2023

Copyright © James Robson, 2023

James Robson has asserted his right under the Copyright, Designs
and Patents Act, 1988, to be identified as Author of this work.

Cover design: Terry Woodley
Cover image: Actress Miriam Hopkins, as Kalonika, in *Lysistrata*, 1930.
Edward Steichen/Condé Nast/Shutterstock.

All rights reserved. No part of this publication may be reproduced or transmitted
in any form or by any means, electronic or mechanical, including photocopying,
recording, or any information storage or retrieval system, without prior
permission in writing from the publishers.

Bloomsbury Publishing Plc does not have any control over, or responsibility for,
any third-party websites referred to or in this book. All internet addresses given
in this book were correct at the time of going to press. The author and publisher
regret any inconvenience caused if addresses have changed or sites have ceased
to exist, but can accept no responsibility for any such changes.

A catalogue record for this book is available from the British Library.

Library of Congress Control Number: 2022941859

ISBN: HB: 978-1-3500-9031-6
        PB: 978-1-3500-9030-9
        ePDF: 978-1-3500-9032-3
        eBook: 978-1-3500-9033-0

Series: Bloomsbury Ancient Comedy Companions

Typeset by RefineCatch Limited, Bungay, Suffolk
Printed and bound in Great Britain

To find out more about our authors and books visit www.bloomsbury.com
and sign up for our newsletters.

Contents

For Owain and Evan
For Mum and Dad

Illustrations

Maps

Timeline of Ancient Events

Note that for Aristophanes' plays, the dramatic festival in Athens at which each was (probably) first performed – i.e. the Lenaea or Dionysia – is given in brackets. (On these festivals, see Chapter 1 Section A.)

514 BCE	Murder of Hipparchus, brother of the tyrant Hippias, by Harmodius and Aristogeiton
510 BCE	Exile of Hippias, tyrant of Athens
508 BCE	Establishment of democracy in Athens
	Occupation of Athens' Acropolis by King Cleomenes of Sparta
492–490 BCE	Persian Wars: first attempted invasion of Greek mainland by the Persians, under Darius
490 BCE	Battle of Marathon
c. 486 BCE	Comedies first staged alongside tragedies at the Great Dionysia festival
480–479 BCE	Persian Wars: second attempted invasion of Greek mainland by the Persians, under Xerxes
480 BCE	Battles of Thermopylae and Artemisium
	Battle of Salamis
478 BCE	Formation of Delian League
464 BCE	Earthquake at Sparta and helot revolt
c. 462 BCE	Athenians dispatch Cimon to Sparta; Cimon's help rejected by Sparta
c. 460–450 BCE	Birth of Aristophanes
454 BCE	Treasury of Delian League moved to Athens
447–432 BCE	Construction of Parthenon on Athens' Acropolis

c. 440 BCE	Comedies first formally staged at the Lenaea festival
431 BCE	Peloponnesian War breaks out between Athens and Sparta
427 BCE	Aristophanes' (lost) *Banqueters* staged (Dionysia)
425 BCE	Aristophanes' *Acharnians* staged (Lenaea)
424 BCE	Aristophanes' *Knights* staged (Lenaea)
423 BCE	Aristophanes' *Clouds* staged (Dionysia)
422 BCE	Aristophanes' *Wasps* staged (Lenaea)
421 BCE	Aristophanes' *Peace* staged (Dionysia)
	Peace of Nicias between Athens and Sparta
418 BCE	Battle of Mantinea
415 BCE	Sicilian Expedition launched by Athens; Mutilation of the Herms
414 BCE	Aristophanes' *Birds* staged (Dionysia)
413 BCE	Sicilian Disaster
411 BCE	Staging of Aristophanes' *Lysistrata* (Lenaea) and *Thesmophoriazusae* (Dionysia)
405 BCE	Aristophanes' *Frogs* staged (Lenaea)
404 BCE	Defeat of Athens in the Peloponnesian War
c. 393–391 BCE	Aristophanes' *Assemblywomen* staged
388 BCE	Aristophanes' *Wealth* staged
c. 386 BCE	Death of Aristophanes

Introduction

Lysistrata was first staged in Athens in 411 BCE at what was one of classical Athens' very darkest hours. The city had recently lost thousands upon thousands of its men in the disastrous Sicilian Expedition and was now at serious risk of losing the Peloponnesian War which it had been fighting against Sparta and her allies for the last twenty years. Political tensions were mounting in Athens, too, which was in constant fear of attack from a Spartan garrison based just north of the city. Yet out of these dire times comes an extraordinary, sparkling play – a fantasy about the women of Greece seizing power and staging a sex strike to force their menfolk to reconcile their differences and live at peace.

In case it needed saying, *Lysistrata* is a lot of fun to be around. It can boast an inventive plot, sassy dialogue, an abundance of dirty jokes and a narrative energy that simply does not let up from beginning to end. Its accessibility for modern audiences is due in part to its tight dramatic structure and its experimentation with the traditions of the comic form, but also, of course, its subject matter. It is for its frank treatment of sex – and especially sexual frustration – that the play tends to be best known. Yet other key themes, such as gender relations, protest, war and peace, are woven into the very fabric of the play, too, and have helped to make *Lysistrata* a particular favourite with audiences over the last century.

This book is aimed at anyone and everyone interested in exploring what *Lysistrata* has to offer. It is written to be as accessible as possible for those who come with little or no knowledge of the classical Greek world but will also, I hope, have lots to offer those studying or teaching the play or, indeed, carrying out academic research on *Lysistrata*. This has not always been an easy balance to strike, but I have aimed to be as straightforward and jargon-free in my writing as possible, whilst not dumbing the material down or shying away from the odd Greek word, challenging concept, or technical term, when I thought it would enrich the discussion. As a reader, it is for you to judge how far I have succeeded in these aims. I have also sought to represent a wide range of scholarly views on the play, and to encourage readers to view such new ideas and interpretations that I offer in this book not as definitive, but as part of a broader set of possible ways to approach and understand the play.

It might be helpful to say a few words about how the book is structured. The introductory material in Chapter 1 (*Lysistrata* in Context: Old Comedy and Athens in 411 BCE) explores the genre of Old Comedy, the historical context of the play, the role of women in classical Athenian society and the production conditions of ancient drama. For anyone new to the play, this material might either be read before reading (or seeing) *Lysistrata* for the first time or, alternatively, following an initial encounter. Chapter 2 (The Action of the Play) provides a walk-through of *Lysistrata* from beginning to end and is intended to allow readers to explore issues of staging and interpretation on a scene-by-scene basis. Chapter 3 (People, Places and Politics) and Chapter 4 (Laughter, Language and Logic) are more synoptic, drawing together the threads of the preceding chapters to consider some of the play's key characters, themes and issues. Lastly, Chapter 5 (*Lysistrata* in the Modern World) explores the rich reception history of the play from the nineteenth century to the modern day. This chapter aims to take the reader on a fascinating journey through the play's reperformance on, and adaptation for, the modern stage, with diversions into the worlds of Aristophanic translation as well as some of the musicals, operas and films that *Lysistrata* has inspired. Chapter titles, section headings and the Index should allow readers to locate the material most relevant to them easily enough, and the suggestions for Further Reading at the end of the book provide further works to peruse and avenues to pursue.

Writing a book can be a solitary slog at the best of times, but the Covid pandemic which hit the UK in 2020 just as I was beginning to put pen to paper (well, finger to keyboard) made this all the more so. My deepest debt as ever goes to my husband, Owain Thomas, for his encouragement, support and all the truly amazing food that lockdown inspired him to cook. My other constant companions were our wonderful son, Evan, and our golden-haired cocker spaniel, Hector, both of whom had a lot of love to give and a lot to communicate in their own ways. I must thank everyone involved in Evan's childcare, too, without whom this book would still be unwritten. The wonderful staff at Henry Fawcett Nursery and Herbert Morrison and Wyvil Schools deserve special mention here, as does the effervescent and ever stylish Marisa Mendez. However, the prize for going way beyond the call of duty goes to my father, Charles Robson, who despite being in his eighties has continued to take on an impressive amount of childcare for the sheer love of it. I know my mother would have wanted to be part of that particular party, too – and, indeed, was part of it right up until the day she died – and she is sorely missed by us all. I also want to give a shout out to Team Classical Studies at the Open University who are simply the best colleagues I could ever ask for and then some, and especially to Christine Plastow for having my back when I have needed to focus on the book. Heartfelt thanks to you all.

Lastly, I want to thank those involved in the production of the book. Lily Mac Mahon at the press has been a pleasure to deal with and Natasha Ellis has done the most awesome job as my image researcher as has Anna Andreopoulou as my indexer. Thanks, too, to Toph Marshall and Niall Slater for believing that someone like me could do a play like *Lysistrata* justice. I just hope I have managed to convey enough of my love and respect for the play in the pages that follow.

Lysistrata in Context: Old Comedy and Athens in 411 BCE

(a) Aristophanes and Old Comedy

Aristophanes was born in Athens sometime around the middle of the fifth century BCE (460–450 BCE, but possibly slightly later) at a time when drama in general and comedy in particular were flourishing in the city. Comic drama had taken longer than tragedy to gain official recognition in Athens, but from 486 BCE comedies began to be staged alongside tragedies as part of the Great Dionysia (also known as the City Dionysia), a religious festival held in honour of Dionysus in Athens in the early spring of each year. From sometime around 440 BCE – when Aristophanes would still have been a boy or young man – comedies began to be formally included in another Dionysiac festival, the Lenaea, where they were joined by tragedies a few years later. With the opportunities, audiences and potential for recognition in Athens growing so rapidly, these must have been exciting times indeed for an aspiring comic playwright.

As with tragedies, comedies were staged at the City Dionysia and the Lenaea on a competitive basis.[1] Playwrights wishing to compete would 'request a chorus' from a civic official called the Archon Eponymous (in the case of the Dionysia) or the Archon Basileus (in the case of the Lenaea) in the summer preceding each year's festival. Those chosen were then allocated a sponsor in the form of a wealthy individual, the play's *chorēgos*, who would cover production costs such as costumes, masks and props as well as paying for the twenty-four members of the chorus to be trained.[2] When it came to being selected for the dramatic competitions at these festivals, established playwrights were presumably at an advantage compared with those who had less experience, which makes all the more appealing the suggestion made by some scholars that Aristophanes initially engaged in some form of comic 'apprenticeship', contributing material to the comedies of other playwrights before authoring plays on his own.[3] Important early landmarks for the young Aristophanes include the staging of his first (full) play, the now lost *Banqueters* in 427 BCE, and the victories he achieved at the Lenaea with his two earliest surviving plays, *Acharnians* (425 BCE) and *Knights* (424 BCE).[4] These were among the forty or so plays that Aristophanes would go on to write in a career spanning over four decades. By the time Aristophanes asked for a chorus for *Lysistrata* in the summer of 412 BCE, ahead of its eventual staging in early 411 BCE, he was already part of Athens' literary and cultural elite – a highly successful playwright and major public figure with a string of comedies to his name.

Lysistrata is an example of 'Old Comedy', a term originating in the ancient world and now used by modern scholars to refer to comic plays written in the fifth century BCE and sometimes extended to include plays composed by Aristophanes (and others) before the playwright's death in or near 386 BCE (later phases being Middle Comedy and New Comedy).[5] The numerous fragments we possess of Old Comedy – as well as the eleven complete plays of Aristophanes that survive, all but two of which date from the fifth century BCE – paint a picture of a constantly evolving genre, whose poets frequently experimented and innovated in an attempt to outdo one another. Indeed, in Aristophanes' plays themselves we often find claims that his comedies are more 'clever' (*sophos*) and 'skilful' (*dexios*) than those of his rivals and full of 'new ideas' (*kainai ideai*), as well as allegations that his innovations were plagiarized by other poets.[6] Yet the traditions of Old Comedy were also strong and members of the theatre audience waiting for *Lysistrata* to begin would doubtless have had certain expectations about the kind of play they were about to see. Old Comic plays characteristically lasted around two hours in performance and contained song and dance, satire and social commentary – as well as conspicuously 'low' elements such as slapstick, word play, risqué jokes and obscenity. *Lysistrata* would prove to be no exception.

Not everything about *Lysistrata* was business as usual, however. For example, when compared with Aristophanes' earlier plays, *Lysistrata* contains strikingly few jibes aimed at public figures in the city. Since ancient scholars of Old Comedy often regarded personal abuse (*onomasti kōmōidein*, 'mocking by name') as a defining feature of Old Comedy, this reluctance to ridicule his fellow citizens is no doubt to be seen as a symptom of the tense political atmosphere in which Aristophanes was working in 411 BCE. Importantly, too, *Lysistrata* may well have been the first comedy to include citizen women as major characters, so an unsuspecting theatregoer might well have been surprised to find a female protagonist in the play in the form of Lysistrata – that is to say, a 'comic heroine' rather than the standard 'comic hero' around whom the plot of Old Comedy more typically revolved. Aside from her sex, however, Lysistrata fits the bill of 'comic hero(ine)' rather well: this is usually a socially marginal figure (most often a poor, older citizen, such as Dicaeopolis in *Acharnians*, but here a citizen wife) who at the beginning of the play is dissatisfied with some aspect of life in contemporary Athens. The comic hero(ine) then seeks to change things for the better by devising a fantastic solution to his or her problems in the form of a 'great idea'.[7] In *Acharnians*, for instance, Dicaeopolis secures peace for himself and his family by means of a private treaty with the Spartans, while Lysistrata achieves the same objective for the whole of Greece through the women's sex strike and seizure of Athens' treasury. In *Lysistrata*, just as in many other Old Comic plays, the hero(ine)'s plans meet obstacles and opposition, but these are eventually overcome, leading to a celebration at the end of the play, involving food and wine and the promise of sex. In support of this standard plot structure – problem, idea, opposition and conflict, resolution, celebration – Old Comic poets made use of a set of traditional elements to structure their plays. These include the prologue (the play's introductory scene), parodos (the entry song of the chorus), *agōn* (a 'contest' between opposing parties), parabasis (a structured set of songs performed by the chorus on its own), and exodos (exit song), each with its own formal conventions. The prologue of *Lysistrata* is used to set the plot in motion, of course, and to introduce some of the key characters of the play, including Lysistrata herself and the Athenian wives. But it also gives a skilled playwright like Aristophanes an important opportunity to capture his audience's attention by providing tantalizing clues about the nature of Lysistrata's 'great idea' ahead of her dramatic revelation of the sex strike plan at line 124 of the play. The parodos involves a further moment of anticipation as the audience waits expectantly to see what form *Lysistrata*'s chorus will take as its members sing and dance their way into view. It is not elaborate costumes, like those worn by the chorus of Aristophanes' *Birds* in 414 BCE, that provide the focus of interest in *Lysistrata*, however; rather the fact that at line 254 (around one-fifth of the way through the play) only twelve chorus members emerge, dressed as old men. The audience must wait until line 319 for the remaining twelve chorus members to join them, this time dressed as old women, for it finally to become clear that Aristophanes has taken the unusual (if not wholly unprecedented) step of dividing his chorus members into two semi-choruses, engaged from the very beginning in a hard-fought battle of the sexes.[8]

One of the remarkable features of *Lysistrata* is how tightly plotted it is compared with many early comedies of Aristophanes and how much he experiments and adapts Old Comedy's conventional building blocks. By way of an *agōn*, for example – traditionally a formally structured 'contest' or 'struggle' between two distinct parties – *Lysistrata* has a loosely configured debate between Lysistrata and the Magistrate (lines 476–607). What is more, this forms just one part of the battle of the sexes that lies at the heart of *Lysistrata*, which is slogged out in a diverse range of ways not only in other episodes in the play (e.g. the seduction scene) but also in many of the play's choral odes, with the old men pitched against the old women. Aristophanes chooses not to include the kind of formal parabasis found in other plays, either: traditionally, this a distinctive (and at times elaborate) set of songs, as part of which the chorus characteristically addresses the audience directly, sometimes speaking in character (e.g. as birds in *Birds*), sometimes expressing what they purport to be the personal views of the playwright. In *Lysistrata*, there is only a very pared down version of this element – the feisty exchanges of the semi-choruses at lines 614–705 of the play – which forms part of a broader trend in Old Comedy for the parabasis to diminish in scale and significance in the late fifth century BCE. But importantly for *Lysistrata*, this paring down allows the semi-choruses to remain fully in character, locked in opposition as old men and old women for the bulk of the play. It is not until peace is brokered towards the end of the play that the chorus finally merges together as one to sing a series of light-hearted songs (1043–71 and 1189–1215). Following this, they fulfil a more conventional role by joining in the general festivities and dancing that precede the upbeat exodos or 'exit song' (1296–1321).

Much of what we know about the structure of Old Comic plays and the development of the genre comes from the comedies of Aristophanes themselves for the simple reason that he is the only representative of Old Comedy whose plays have survived in anything other than fragmentary form. Indeed, a remarkable number of Aristophanes' plays have come down to us: eleven comedies in total stretching from *Acharnians* (425 BCE) to *Wealth* (388 BCE), representing around a quarter of his output (this is a far higher proportion than the three great tragedians of classical Athens, Aeschylus, Sophocles and even Euripides can boast). This is partly an accident of survival, partly attributable to later generations being inclined to see Aristophanes as the preeminent poet of Old Comedy, and partly because the plays were seen by ancient scholars as a particularly rich source of standard Attic (i.e. Athenian) Greek as spoken in the classical era which therefore merited preservation.

As for the text of *Lysistrata* that we possess, this essentially forms part of a manuscript tradition stretching from the classical era itself to a time when printing presented an alternative way of preserving and distributing the text: in the case of *Lysistrata*, the first published version of the play appeared in Italy in 1515–16. Not that the manuscript tradition is particularly rich: whereas Aristophanes' best-preserved play, *Wealth*, survives in about 150 manuscripts, and *Knights* in thirty, the figure for *Lysistrata* is just eight (an indication of the play's relative lack of popularity during the Byzantine era).[9] It should be said, too, that we cannot be certain what the text that has come down to us represents: maybe an acting script for the original production or a later restaging of the play; maybe the author's edited version for circulation; but maybe something else.[10] In its modern, edited form, *Lysistrata* comprises 1,321 lines of Greek – and it is these line numbers which are used in this book to refer to passages in the play. The bulk of the play is composed in iambic trimeters, a poetic metre which, Aristotle tells us, is the most 'colloquial' (*lektikos*); that is to say, closest to the rhythms of everyday speech (*Poetics* 1449a24–5). But a rich array of other poetic metres feature in the play, too, from no-nonsense anapaests (e.g. the metre of Cinesias' lament when he is cheated of sex: lines 954–79, which would probably have been chanted as recitative) and high-flown dactylic hexameters (e.g. Lysistrata's oracle: lines 770–6) to the metrically complex rhythms found in some of the play's choral odes or the celebratory songs sung by the Spartan at the end of the play (1247–72, 1279–94 and 1296–1321). Important elements of *Lysistrata*, then, would have been its music and the choreography that accompanied it. In addition to the sixty-five lines sung by the Spartan, the chorus sing over 200 lines as well; or in other words, around one-fifth of the play's performance time would have been given over to song and dance.[11]

The manuscripts of *Lysistrata* that we possess raise an inevitable set of questions. These concern issues such as the accuracy of the Greek (since the text will have been copied and recopied a number of times); the staging of the play and use of props (since there are no original stage directions); and, importantly for *Lysistrata*, the attribution of lines to speakers (since manuscripts often mark a change of speaker simply by means of either a double line or a long dash, a detail that can potentially be misplaced or accidently omitted by a scribe).[12] These questions have in turn led to some lively scholarly debates, e.g. concerning the identity of speakers in the final scene of the play: is it Lysistrata who oversees the reunification of the husbands and wives at lines 1273–8 or someone else? The scholia (i.e. the comments of ancient scholars which came to be written in the margins of manuscripts) are sometimes helpful here, since they often represent attempts to elucidate the text for its readers; but since it is not always easy to distinguish between sound knowledge and educated guesses, these have also prompted some animated discussions amongst modern scholars. For example, are we to believe the scholiast who claims that the original play would have ended with a traditional hymn to Athena? Opinion is divided.[13]

(b) Contemporary Athens: The Peloponnesian War and the events of 411 BCE

In 411 BCE, the year that *Lysistrata* was first performed in Athens, the city's fortunes were in a precarious state. Since 431 BCE much of the

Greek-speaking world had been locked in the Peloponnesian War, a bruising conflict which saw Athens and its allies pitched against a confederacy of city-states led by its great adversary, Sparta. Following a fragile peace treaty brokered in 421 BCE (the Peace of Nicias) and a decisive victory for Sparta in a land battle in 418 BCE (the Battle of Mantinea), an uneasy stalemate had prevailed, with Sparta consolidating its powerbase in the Peloponnese and Athens ruling over what was essentially an empire, an array of allied and subject city-states, made up of islands and coastal towns in the Aegean and beyond.

The event that brought the two sides into open conflict again was the Sicilian Expedition, a military campaign of enormous scale, launched by Athens in 415 BCE in an ambitious attempt to conquer the island of Sicily (referred to at lines 390–7 of the play). The awe-inspiring fleet that set sail for Sicily was, according to the historian Thucydides, 'the most costly and finest looking . . . that up to that time had ever come from a single city' (Thucydides 6.31). But when the Athenian armada reached Sicily, the main advocate of the Expedition and one of the fleet's three commanders, the flamboyant and charismatic aristocrat Alcibiades, found that he had been recalled to Athens on suspicion of being involved in both a parody of the Eleusinian Mysteries (secret religious rites connected with Demeter and Persephone) and an incident known as the Mutilation of the Herms. This was a nocturnal romp, possibly carried out by members of an aristocratic drinking club, which saw many of the traditional stone statues of Hermes that stood outside Athenian households have their protruding phalluses knocked off (this incident is alluded to at *Lysistrata* 1094; see also Figure 1.2, where an example of a herm can be found on the left-hand side of the scene). On his way back to Athens, Alcibiades fled and subsequently offered his services to the Spartans.

Alcibiades' defection was just one of the many setbacks, ill omens and poor strategic decisions that dogged the Sicilian Expedition from

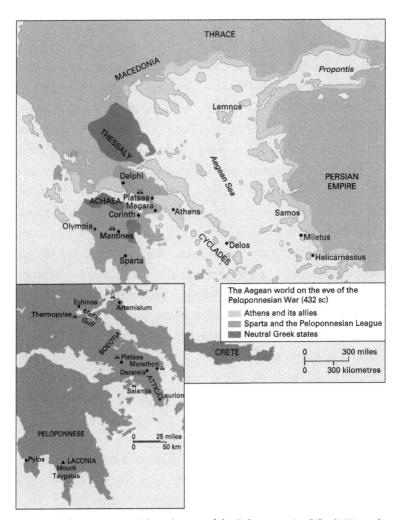

Map 1.1 The Aegean world on the eve of the Peloponnesian War (432 BCE).

the very beginning. The venture ended in a disaster of historic proportions: by the late summer of 413 BCE, hardly anything of the Athenian fleet remained and nearly all the men that Athens had despatched to the island had either been killed, captured or sold into slavery: over 200 ships and 30,000 men in total. For the audience of

Lysistrata, this would have been painful, recent history: there can have been few Athenians who had not lost a family member on the island.

The colossal loss of life and near-total destruction of the Athenian fleet in the Sicilian Expedition left the city hugely vulnerable. Key allied states began to abandon Athens (including the island of Melos, mentioned at line 108 of the play) and in the Eastern Aegean the mighty Persia looked set to make a decisive intervention in the conflict. Persian governors not only made efforts to bring Athenian-allied cities in Asia Minor under Persia's control, but also entered negotiations with Sparta about forming an alliance. Closer to home, a Spartan garrison stationed at Deceleia, just 20 kilometres or 13 miles to the north of Athens, evidently caused huge anxiety in the city (at *Lysistrata* 555–64 we hear of men doing shopping in their armour so as to be ready to respond to a surprise military attack). Importantly, this garrison also served to confine Athenians within their fortified walls, thus cutting them off from both their farmland and a key source of their wealth, the silver mines at Laurion. But Sparta and her allies failed to capitalize on Athens' weakness, and the new Athenian fleet, built using emergency reserves, even managed to score some minor successes by reconquering some of the allied states that had revolted. By the winter of 412/11 BCE, as Aristophanes and his cast and chorus rehearsed and refined *Lysistrata*, the chances of Athens securing a good outcome in the Peloponnesian War must certainly have seemed low; but, against all odds, the city was still in the game.

What could possibly be the solution to Athens' problems? *Lysistrata* provides a particularly appealing answer here: a pan-Hellenic peace which sees the warring parties put their differences to one side and unite against their old, common enemy, Persia. But palatable solutions in the real world were less forthcoming.

The events of late 412 BCE and the early part of 411 BCE, just prior to *Lysistrata*'s performance, are not easy to untangle. One public figure mentioned in *Lysistrata* who was set to play an influential role in

Athenian affairs is Peisander, a general stationed on the island of Samos. He had probably arrived in Athens as part of a delegation in late 412 BCE, a few weeks before the staging of *Lysistrata* – which most likely took place at the Lenaea festival in early February BCE (see Section E, below). Later that year Peisander would go on to propose to Athens' Assembly radical changes to the city's constitution – i.e. to turn it from a democracy to an oligarchy – as part of a bold plan to secure support from Persia with the help of the exiled aristocrat Alcibiades, who was now seeking to return to Athens. There is no indication in *Lysistrata* that this plan was already public knowledge, however; Peisander is spoken of as an agitator looking to profit from the public purse, but not as someone seeking radical reform and an alliance with Athens' old enemy (lines 490–2). The fact that, just a few weeks after *Lysistrata* was performed, a drastic change to Athens' form of government could be proposed is nevertheless highly suggestive. These were fraught times and so it should perhaps come as no surprise that characters in *Lysistrata* voice the need to 'save' (*sōizein*) Athens: indeed, this was most likely a political buzzword of the day.[14] In the summer of 411 BCE, the oligarchs would finally succeed in overturning Athens' democratic government, leading to the bloody, if short-lived, Rule of the Four Hundred. *Lysistrata* clearly offered its spectators an escapist fantasy at a time when political intrigues were brewing and the future of Athens could hardly have been more uncertain.

(c) *Lysistrata*'s long view: The Persian Wars and inter-state relations in the fifth century BCE

While very much a product of the turbulent times in which it was produced, *Lysistrata* also reveals a remarkable preoccupation with past military glories and the common history shared by Athens and Sparta. The historical events referred to in the play stretch back over a century to the final years of the rule of Hippias, the tyrant of Athens, who was eventually driven into exile in 510 BCE. Indeed, the old men of the chorus even claim personal involvement in the tumultuous events surrounding the establishment of Athenian democracy in 508 BCE, when they offer their somewhat exaggerated recollections of the attempt by King Cleomenes of Sparta to intervene in Athenian domestic affairs at that time (at lines 272–80, they seemingly claim to have laid siege to Cleomenes on Athens' Acropolis for six years, when in reality he departed after two days).

The Persian Wars of 492–490 BCE and 480–479 BCE – the conflicts that played such a key role in shaping the identity and politics of Greek city-states in the fifth century BCE – feature particularly prominently in the play. Significantly, the old men of the chorus are Marathonomachai, veterans of the Battle of Marathon, the military encounter which spelt the end of Persia's first attempted invasion of mainland Greece and which was regularly evoked in classical Athenian culture as the city's finest hour. Not that many Marathonomachai could plausibly have been alive when *Lysistrata* was first staged, since it was in 490 BCE that a hugely outnumbered Greek army, made up almost entirely of Athenian soldiers, attacked and defeated the invading Persian forces at Marathon (a coastal town around 40 kilometres or 25 miles from Athens). Routed, the enemy fled to their ships and soon afterwards sailed back to Persia. The historian Herodotus tells us that the Athenian dead at Marathon numbered just 192 (with their allies, the Plataeans suffering minor losses, too, and an unknown number of Athenian slaves also amongst the casualties), whereas the Persian battlefield casualties numbered 6,400 (Herodotus 6.117). The dead were cremated where they fell and a monument later erected in their honour: this is the so-called 'Trophy of the Four Towns' referred to at line 285 of *Lysistrata* as a symbol of the old men's military valour.[15]

One of the distinctive features of the Persian Wars was the co-operative nature of the Greek campaign. While some Greek city-states capitulated to Persia and many others chose to remain neutral during the attempted invasions, an alliance of states, amongst which Athens and Sparta were the key players, worked together each time to repel the threat posed by their mighty Persian neighbour. Marathon may have been a particularly Athenian victory (the Spartan army mobilized but arrived a day too late, having been detained through their observance of a festival of Apollo), but the Spartans were more prominent in other encounters. These include two battles which took place in the late summer of 480 BCE during Persia's second attempted invasion, namely Artemisium (a major, if somewhat indecisive, naval battle which saw heavy losses on both the allied Greek and Persian sides) and Thermopylae (where 300 Spartan hoplites – along with allied troops from Thespiae and Thebes – were notoriously slaughtered while defending a narrow pass): these form the subject of the Spartan's song at lines 1247–72 of the play. With the loss of Thermopylae, mainland Greece became exposed, and the Persians marched on Athens. Most Athenians abandoned their city, fleeing to the Peloponnese or nearby islands. However, the few that chose to remain barricaded themselves on the Acropolis, to which the Persians then set fire when they arrived. A turning point was soon to come, however, in the form of the Battle of Salamis – a decisive naval victory for the allied Greek forces in late 480 BCE. This battle is also alluded to by *Lysistrata*'s chorus of old men: they recall the actions of the talented and feisty Artemisia, Queen of Halicarnassus, who alone of the Persian commanders excelled in battle that day (line 675).[16]

The Persian Wars were to have a profound and lasting effect on Greek inter-state relations in the fifth century BCE. Eager to avert the threat of a third invasion, many maritime city-states entered into an alliance with Athens, whose prowess in the Persian Wars, relative wealth and sizeable navy marked it out as a natural leader and defender of the seas. This alliance, the Delian League, was formed in 478 BCE and named after Delos, the island on which the allies' oaths were sworn and where its treasury was located. Increasingly, as the years wore on, more and more allied states made their contribution to the League in cash rather than ships, with Athens the main financial beneficiary. Eventually, in 454 BCE, the treasury was moved to Athens itself (during the Peloponnesian War the city's monetary reserves were located on the Acropolis, which is why its seizure is so key to Lysistrata's plan). The League had effectively become an Athenian Empire whose funds – referred to by the old women of the chorus as Athens' rightful inheritance from the Persian Wars (lines 652–3) – not only allowed Athens to maintain a powerful navy but also to fund public works, including, from 447 BCE, the construction of the Parthenon (the temple of Athena, in her guise of the 'virgin' goddess or *parthenos*) as well as other buildings on the Acropolis. Importantly, too, this income from Athens' allies-cum-subjects underpinned the city's radical democracy, since citizen men could be paid a fee to undertake civic activities such as attending the Assembly, serving in the navy and sitting on juries (all of which could provide important sources of income for Athens' poor; indeed, the old men of the play are envisaged as supporting themselves financially by serving as jurors: *Lysistrata* 380 and 624). Sparta, a deeply conservative monarchy with a formidable reputation for military prowess on land, emerged as Greece's other great power, standing at the head of a rival alliance of city-states, the Peloponnesian League. Tensions between the powerful blocs presided over by Athens and Sparta simmered throughout the fifth century BCE, giving rise to sporadic skirmishes, conflicts and finally, of course, the Peloponnesian War of 431–404 BCE.

(d) Women in classical Athens

While it is not always easy to disentangle historical reality from the exaggeration, jokes and distorted logic typical of Old Comedy,

Aristophanes' plays nevertheless provide a rich resource for studying women's lives in classical Athens. As was standard in the ancient Mediterranean, sexual roles were clearly demarcated in the city, with women's legal and political rights extremely limited. A citizen household was typically headed by a man, for example, who acted as the legal custodian (*kurios*) of both his wife and any unmarried females in his household (a state of affairs which meant that even physical and sexual violence towards a wife might essentially go unchallenged, as we find out at lines 160–4, 225–8 and 516–20). Women were also excluded from Athens' political institutions such as the Assembly, which was the sole preserve of citizen men (this is highlighted at lines 507–20, where Lysistrata describes how women are forced to keep quiet while men allegedly make bad public policy decisions). One important element of the play, then – and a prominent source of its humour – is the topsy-turvy nature of the world into which the audience is plunged. In *Lysistrata*, women abandon their households and husbands and take charge of the public domain, assuming roles such as orator and civic leader (in the case of Lysistrata) and spirited warriors (in the case of the old women), which would have been unthinkable in the real world of contemporary Athens. And just as women take on masculine roles, so are the men of the play feminized. The Magistrate is at one point made to sport typically female accoutrements, such as Lysistrata's veil and a basket for working wool (535–7); Cinesias takes on the task of caring for his baby (if only momentarily: 877–908); and the younger men become weakened by their overpowering sexual urges, having lost their sexual autonomy as a result of the sex strike.

One of the remarkable achievements of the play is how Aristophanes makes this topsy-turvy state of affairs, including the concept of female rule, seem almost logical. For instance, Lysistrata says that a skill learnt by wives in the household (*oikos*), namely the management of domestic finances, might also be used by women to run the city (*polis*): managing of the state economy is essentially the same task as running a household budget, she suggests, just on a larger scale (493–6). In a similar vein, in her famous wool-working metaphor (line 573–86), Lysistrata proposes that the city's problems can be solved in the same way that women turn an unruly skein of wool into a woven cloak: again the suggestion is that domestic, female skills can usefully be applied to running the city (see also Chapter 2 Section D and Chapter 3 Section C). The domestic sphere which is typically the domain of women is brought outside into the public realm in other ways, too. The most visually striking example of this, perhaps, is the makeshift bedroom created by Myrrhine on the slopes of the Acropolis for her husband, Cinesias, in the play's seduction scene.

Another way in which the idea of women in charge is evoked and normalized in the play is through Aristophanes' use of mythical and historical paradigms. The old men of the chorus liken the pugnacious old women to Amazons, a particularly apposite comparison, given that these mythical female warriors were said to have besieged the Athenian Acropolis (an event commemorated on the painted marble metopes of the Parthenon – as well as in public paintings by the artist Micon, as we are reminded at lines 678–9).[17] Also evoked is the myth of the Lemnian Women (299), who murdered their husbands and took control of their island (like the women of *Lysistrata*, the rule of women on Lemnos was to prove temporary: their marriage to the Argonauts eventually saw them return to their traditional roles as wives).[18] The role of Artemisia, Queen of Halicarnassus, in the Battle of Salamis, which is recalled by the old men of the chorus (675), likewise serves to remind the audience of an historical example of successful female leadership (see Section C, above).

The connection between 'respectable' citizen women and the household was strong for classical Athenians, with a notional ideal – especially for an upper-class woman or a girl of marriageable age – being for her to remain at home, protected even from the gaze of men (the speaker in a fourth-century BCE legal case claims, albeit somewhat improbably, that his nieces 'live so respectfully that they are shamed at being seen even by members of the family': Lysias 3.6). In *Lysistrata* we find detailed some of the tasks that women performed at home – such as the care of husbands, looking after of children and wool-working (17–19, 535–7) – which taken together neatly exemplify the classical Athenian archetype of the virtuous, loyal and industrious wife and mother. But even 'respectable' women and girls would have had legitimate reasons to leave the house and we are reminded of some of these during the play, too, such as the fetching of water (the old women appear with their pitchers in the parodos) and involvement in religious activities. Indeed, women's role in both public and private religion is particularly prominent, from participation in wedding and funerary ritual (378, 599–604) to more riotous forms of worship (the cults of Bacchus, Pan and Genetyllis mentioned at the very beginning of the play: lines 1–3) and the contribution – usually by upper-class girls – to prominent civic rituals in honour of goddesses such as Athena and Artemis (641–7).

Of course, not every woman belonged to a household that was sufficiently wealthy to enable her to remain at home, economically inactive. Many women were compelled by poverty or other circumstances to work outside the house, and the number doing so during the Peloponnesian War would have only increased owing to the death or absence of male breadwinners.[19] At lines 456–8, Lysistrata uses some inventive compound-words to call on two notoriously hardened groups of female workers, namely women who sell their wares in the Athenian marketplace and female innkeepers, to assist her in the battle against the Magistrate and his Scythian archers: 'Show yourselves, you market-place-breed-of-porridge-and-vegetable-saleswomen! Advance, you garlicky-landlady-breadsellers!' The old women of the chorus are also far from genteel and display much more independence than the younger wives, reflecting the greater freedoms enjoyed by women whose child-bearing years were behind them – as well as the reputation for toughness that such women enjoyed.[20] In the play, these older women threaten, swear at, fight and overwhelm men, playing their own distinctive role in Lysistrata's grand scheme. As for non-citizen women, these are largely absent from the play, though a slave does appear in the prologue (an enslaved Scythian woman, who brings accoutrements for the swearing of the oath at lines 184 and 199). There is the fantasy figure of Reconciliation, too, who appears at line 1115 to be ogled and fondled by the Athenian and Spartan men. Reconciliation is essentially characterized as a sexually alluring *hetaira* (prostitute), a profession that was typically the preserve of immigrant and enslaved women in classical Athens.[21]

Lysistrata also affords a glimpse of stereotypes and prejudices about women – indeed, Aristophanes exploits to great effect the typical Old Comic characterization of young women as wine-loving and sex-mad. In the oath-swearing scene, for example, the wives appear to be far more interested in the cup and wine jar over which they are swearing than the oath itself ('Let me be the first to swear, ladies!', 207) and the Magistrate is quick to associate women's feistiness with their consumption of wine (466). But as a play whose plot has a sex strike at its heart, it is women's supposed fondness for sex that takes centre stage. The women initially reject the idea of the strike ('Let the war carry on!' 129–30) and Calonice is also seen to struggle when swearing the oath to abstain from sex ('Oh no! My knees are giving way, Lysistrata', 215–16). Later in the play, in a scene that plays on yet another stereotypical characteristic of women – namely, deceitfulness – a series of women attempt to escape from the Acropolis, each with a thinly veiled excuse that suggests a sexual motive ('At home I've got some Milesian fleeces ... I'll come back right away, just as soon as I've ... *spread* them on the bed', 729–32). Lastly, the rampant misogyny of the old men gives a lively impression of some of the more extreme opinions that might have been voiced about women in real life. Women are described as 'shameless' (369, 1015), 'wild animals' (468) and a 'blatant evil we've reared in our homes' (261–2).

As outlined above (Section A), 411 BCE was most likely a breakthrough year for the portrayal of women in Old Comedy: this was possibly the first time that citizen wives were portrayed in major roles in a play. Intriguingly, too, Aristophanes staged not one but two plays that year with female citizens at their heart: *Lysistrata* and *Thesmophoriazusae* (one at the Lenaea and one at the Great Dionysia). But what might have prompted Aristophanes to innovate in this way? One answer is no doubt to be found at an artistic level. Taking inspiration from tragedy, where female figures had long been prominent, and building on previous comic experiments with female characters and choruses, Aristophanes simply took the next logical step by creating his first comic heroine, Lysistrata, whose fantastic plan requires the involvement of other citizen wives. In this light, *Lysistrata* might be seen as an evolution in the genre of Old Comedy rather than as a revolution: a play whose innovations have their roots in previous theatrical experiments and traditions. But there is surely more to the story than this. Importantly, the use of citizen women as central characters also allows for an exploration of the impact of war in the domestic sphere – at the level of the *oikos* (household) and not just the *polis* (city-state). This technique can be traced back as far as Homer, where in Book 6 of the *Iliad* the action moves from the battlefield outside Troy to the besieged city itself, including its homes and its women. Indeed, we even find an echo of *Iliad* Book 6 in *Lysistrata* when the Magistrate quotes the words that the Trojan Prince, Hector, addresses to his wife, Andromache, as he departs for the battlefield: 'war is men's concern' (*Iliad* 6.492; *Lysistrata* 520). Lysistrata turns this assertion on its head, however, declaring that 'war is women's concern' (538). As she powerfully states, war leaves mothers bereft of their sons, deprives wives of their husbands when they are absent on campaign and robs young women of the all-important opportunity to marry (588–97; motherhood and marriage typically playing a crucial role in citizen women's identity and status).

Since women bemoan the absence of men and the disruption of household routines in the play's prologue, it seems likely that in *Lysistrata* Aristophanes has captured some genuine, contemporary sources of female discontent. After all, with many husbands, sons and fathers dead, especially after the colossal casualties of the Sicilian Disaster, and with many others away on campaign, life for most women in Athens will have changed – sometimes subtly, sometimes dramatically – and those who were living in straitened circumstances, or who had little left to lose, might well have had cause to voice their grievances. In this light, it is tempting to see *Lysistrata* as a response by Aristophanes to emerging social tensions and topical concerns about the changing role of women – albeit in the form of a play with a fantastic plotline whose ending sees the traditional gender roles restored, with men at home once again, in charge of both their wives and households.

There may be a further factor, too, behind Aristophanes' choice of women to critique the policies being pursued by Athens' leaders in 411 BCE. The extraordinarily tense political situation that prevailed at the time would no doubt have made the kind of pointed ridicule and searing criticism of public figures found in Aristophanes' earlier plays risky to say the least. Indeed, the bloody events of the summer of that year show just how perilous it could be to make oneself prominent on the wrong side of a political debate. For a comic playwright, then, a female character may have provided an offbeat and therefore more safe-seeming vehicle for exploring misgivings about the conduct of the war and for offering the city advice – as, of course, Lysistrata repeatedly does.

(e) Staging *Lysistrata* in 411 BCE

While there is no ancient testimony to tell us at which of Athens' two dramatic festivals *Lysistrata* was staged, the firm scholarly consensus is that it was first performed at the Lenaea, which in 411 BCE would have fallen in early February (Gamelion 8–11 of the Athenian calendar).[22] Disappointingly little is known about this mid-winter festival, but what has been established by scholars suggests that, in addition to comic and tragic contests, it involved various religious rites in honour of Dionysus, such as a procession and animal sacrifice, seemingly focused around the Lenaion, a sanctuary of Dionysus of unknown location either in or near the city of Athens.[23] Strictly speaking, our ignorance about the Lenaea even extends to the location of its dramatic contests in the late fifth century BCE.[24] However, the most likely venue for these is the Theatre of Dionysus on the southern slopes of the Acropolis, where the plays written for the City Dionysia, Athens' other major dramatic contest, were also staged. The Theatre of Dionysus would certainly have provided a fitting backdrop for *Lysistrata* given that much of the play's action takes place on or near the Acropolis. For an audience sitting in this theatre, a number of locations mentioned in the play, such as the gateway to the Acropolis (the Propylaea), the shrine of Chloe and Pan's Grotto (265, 835, 721 and 911), would all have been less than 200 metres (200 yards) away.

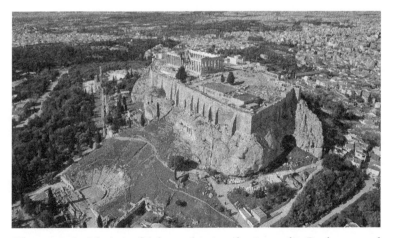

Figure 1.1 Aerial view of Athens, showing the Acropolis, Parthenon and Theatre of Dionysus.

Lysistrata would have been staged in a large, mainly wooden, open-air theatre. It was not until the mid-fourth century BCE, some sixty years after *Lysistrata* was produced, that work began on the project to build the Theatre of Dionysus in stone, some of the remains of which can still be seen today (despite later adaptations and additions, most notably in the Roman period: see Figure 1.1. The capacity of the earlier, fifth-century BCE theatre has proven to be a particularly rich source of scholarly debate, with estimates ranging from 3,700 to 7,000 – an enormous figure when compared with most modern, indoor theatre audiences.[25] Given the distinct possibility that the spectators in the Theatre of Dionysus itself were joined by other onlookers, perched on the upper slopes of the Acropolis beyond the back row of the theatre (and who thereby avoided payment of the entrance fee),[26] the reference to an audience size of 10,000 that appears in Aristophanes' *Frogs* would seem a plausible ball park estimate.[27] As befits a civic and religious occasion, an audience of this kind would inevitably have contained a rich cross-section of Athenian society – in terms of age, civic status, profession, political leanings, and so on – yet it also seems likely, as has been argued by Alan Sommerstein, that the audience sitting in the theatre itself would have been skewed in favour of wealthy, educated and socially elite Athenians.[28] Particularly controversial is the question of whether women were present in the theatre. If there is a scholarly consensus here, it is that they did attend, but only in modest numbers.[29]

Whilst largely nestling in the same space as its fourth-century BCE counterpart, the raked seating of the Theatre of Dionysus known to Aristophanes would have been made up not of elegantly curving rows of stone seats, but rather of straight wooden benches (*ikria*) laid out around the *orchēstra* – the large, central 'dancing space' which, amongst other things, provided a location for the twenty-four members of a comic chorus to perform their choreographed sequences. As in the later stone theatre, behind the *orchēstra* and facing the spectators stood the *skēnē*, a wooden stage building which boasted a large pair of inwardly opening double doors at its centre: for much of the action of *Lysistrata*, these serve as the entrance to the Athenian Acropolis. Characters might emerge through these central doors – just as Lysistrata and the other younger wives do once the women are stationed in the Acropolis – but, alternatively, actors could arrive and depart in the same manner as the chorus, namely using one of the two *parodoi*, the long passages which lay at either side of the stage building. This is how Lampito and the other non-Athenian women arrive at the beginning of the play, for example. Importantly, too, the roof of the *skēnē* could double up as an acting space: Lysistrata appears here, as if on the walls of the Acropolis, when she spies and then talks to Myrrhine's husband, Cinesias (lines 829–65).

In the absence of decisive literary or archaeological evidence, many details about the production conditions of fifth-century BCE drama remain contentious, such as the shape of the *orchēstra* in Theatre of Dionysus (was it essentially circular like that of the later stone theatre or more oblong-shaped?), the number of doors in the *skēnē* and, in particular, whether or not there was a stage.[30] A number of vase paintings of comic scenes from the late fifth and early fourth centuries BCE, such as Figure 1.3, depict a low, wooden stage connected to the *orchēstra* by a short flight of wooden steps. While it is important to bear in mind both when and where these theatrical vases were produced – most post-date Aristophanes and were largely produced in Greek-speaking communities in Southern Italy rather than in Athens itself – scholars who support the idea of a stage in fifth-century BCE Athens emphasize the close links between the two dramatic traditions.[31] So why doubt the presence of a stage? Well, some fifth-century BCE theatres seem to have functioned without one – such as the rectangular theatre at Thorikos, 40 kilometres (25 miles) from Athens – and it is also arguable that the modestly proportioned stage we find depicted on vases would have been too small to accommodate

some of the larger crowd scenes found in comedy. But these objections
largely disappear if we envisage the *orchēstra* as an area used by the
chorus and characters alike, with the stage serving as the location for
discrete sequences in each play rather than as an area to which the
actors were confined.

Also relevant when trying to conceptualize the staging of
Aristophanes' plays are studies of ancient theatrical space which
highlight the importance of the line between the central doors of
the *skēnē* and the centre point of the *orchēstra* for commanding the
attention of the audience both visually and aurally.[32] Certainly, the
area around the *skēnē* doors (including the centre of the stage, if there
was one) must have provided a key location for the action of *Lysistrata*,
since for much of the play these represent the barred gates of the
Acropolis. That said, the play's ancient director (*didaskalos*),
Aristophanes' long-standing collaborator, Callistratus, might plausibly
have chosen to bring his actors closer to the centre of the *orchēstra* for
other key scenes in the play. As for the number of speaking actors,
Aristophanes and his fellow comic playwrights display more flexibility
than fifth-century BCE tragedians who generally limit themselves to
just three. Some sequences in *Lysistrata* clearly require a fourth
speaking actor, such as the prologue where Lysistrata, the Athenian
wives Calonice and Myrhhine, and the Spartan Lampito all have
speaking roles, and some scholars have even suggested that there
might even have been a role for a fifth speaking actor in the play
(albeit one who delivered just a handful of lines).[33] Minor parts, such
as the women from Boeotia and Corinth in the prologue, would have
been played by silent extras.

Classical Greek theatre was, as Oliver Taplin puts it, very much a
'theatre of the mind', the open air setting and rudimentary technology
available to ancient theatre practitioners requiring the audience to
imagine the scene changes and stage effects characteristic of much
modern Western theatre.[34] But the physicality of Old Comedy also

Figure 1.2 The 'Goose Play' vase, Apulian red-figure bell-krater, depicting comic athletes wrestling, *c.* 400–380 BCE.

made it a highly visual genre, with elements such as slapstick, staged conflict, choral dance and the deployment of eye-catching costumes and props serving to create a sense of spectacle for the audience. Vase paintings such as Figure 1.2 (the 'Goose Play' vase) provide a useful impression not only of the larger-than-life costumes that Athenian comic actors might have worn in the late fifth century BCE but also of the ways actors might have interacted with the theatrical space and props. Here two characters, a dark-haired man and a white-haired man, assume lively poses as they prepare to wrestle: on the left of the scene the younger man props up a stick with his finger, having placed his cloak and oil flask on the head of a herm (a small statue of Hermes, complete with an erect phallus). Meanwhile, the older man on the right, who has also stripped off in anticipation of the wrestling bout, pours oil on his hands from another flask to rub onto his skin. Each character is in fact 'stage naked', wearing a wrinkled body suit (the

limits of which are depicted by lines at the actors' feet and ankles and
by the younger man's scooped neckline) as well as the padded belly,
chest and rump typical of comic actors. They also sport masks that
cover the whole head, complete with hair, gaping mouth and distorted
comic features. Lastly, attached to the waist of each actor is an oversized, dangling, leather phallus: when characters are clothed, these
often swung visibly below their short cloaks (see Figure 1.3). In the
later episodes of *Lysistrata*, these conventional pieces of stage attire
feature prominently, reconfigured as upward-pointing, oversize
erections – a visible symbol of the physical effect on the younger men
of the women's sex strike. The items perched on the right-hand side of
the elevated stage in Figure 1.2 – two baskets containing baby goats
and a (seemingly live) goose – also serve as a useful reminder of both
the importance of individual props and also the way in which objects
can accumulate on stage in comedy during fast-moving scenes. In
Lysistrata, the cup used for the oath-swearing scene (in the prologue)
and the old women's pitchers (in the parodos) both briefly become a
symbolic focus of attention, and the objects brought outside by
Myrrhine during the seduction scene as she tantalizes her husband
with promises of sex – including a mattress, blanket, pillows and
perfumed oil – gradually pile up in a hectic comic sequence full of
humorous potential.[35]

Over bodysuits like those depicted on the 'Goose Play' vase
(Figure 1.2), actors would have normally worn costumes appropriate
to their character-type, such as a young citizen (in the case of Cinesias,
for example), or an older man (such as the Magistrate). Some examples
of the variety of male masks and costumes can be seen in Figure 1.3
where, alongside a white-haired man and two dark-haired older men,
we find a younger man seemingly dressed as a tragic rather than
comic character. Actors playing female characters would similarly
have worn masks and clothing to match the parts they were playing
(see Figure 1.4). Importantly in a theatrical tradition where there was

Figure 1.3 The Choregos vase, Apulian red-figure bell-krater, attributed to the Choregos Painter, *c.* 380 BCE.

Figure 1.4 Apulian bell-krater illustrating a scene from Aristophanes' *Thesmophoriazusae, c.* 370 BCE.

a limited number of speaking actors, masks and costumes allowed the same actor to play a variety of characters in a play. They also provided important visual cues to the audience about the characters the moment they came into view, such as their sex, age, status (free or enslaved) and even ethnicity. In *Lysistrata*, for example, the garments worn by the Athenian men and women would have differed from those of the Spartans and other Peloponnesians. One intriguing question is how Lysistrata herself might have been costumed: did her hair and clothing suggest that she was young, mature or somewhere in between?

Needless to say, the production conditions of the classical Greek theatre must have demanded a special set of skills from actors. The clear delivery of lines through the aperture of the mask – both spoken and sung – must have required both natural ability and considerable training. Actors must also have employed techniques which their modern Western counterparts experimenting with masked acting only learn through trial and error: how to use 'dynamic poses' to bring a character to life and 'meaningful gestures of both head and body' to convey a particular mood, attitude or reaction.[36] *Lysistrata* would have provided a distinct set of challenges for comic actors, too, given the unusually large number of substantial female characters. To bring this play to life, the male actors would presumably have had to dig deep, drawing on any previous experience they had of travesty acting to develop effective ways of portraying the play's diverse cast of women.

It is worth considering briefly the ways in which Aristophanes' script specifically caters for, and makes a virtue of, the production conditions of the fifth-century BCE theatre. One simple technique that Aristophanes uses frequently, for example, is to have one character announce the arrival of another. This conveniently buys time for the actor to arrive at the centre of the action, whilst serving the important purpose of informing the audience of the newcomer's identity (lines 5–6 and 77).

Lysistrata   . . . here's my neighbour coming out. Greetings,
Calonice!

Myrrhine   . . . and look, here comes Lampito now, in fact.

In a large-scale theatre, it also makes sense that characters regularly
verbalize details of clothing, personal appearance or staging, thereby
allowing spectators to visualize things that they might not be able to
see. Sometimes the words of speakers simply reflect the stage business
that is taking place at the time, such as when Lysistrata and the women
force their female accoutrements onto the Magistrate (lines 532–5).

Lysistrata   . . . take this here veil from me – here you go – and
put it round your head. And then be quiet!

First Old Woman   And take this wool basket, too.

At other times, however, emotions are skilfully projected onto a character's
unmoving mask, with visual cues, such as posture and movement, no
doubt reinforcing the verbal cues in the text. Near the beginning of the
play, for instance, Calonice describes the look that Lysistrata supposedly
has on her face, addressing her as follows (lines 7–8):

Calonice   What's made you so distraught? Don't look sullen, my
child (*teknon*). Knitted brows aren't a good look on you.

In a similar vein, the sheer size of the fifth-century BCE theatre space
makes it feasible for mimed or invented details to be described as if they
are really taking place. These might include the dousing of the old men
with water (at line 382 of the parodos) and certainly the removal of a
gnat from the eye of the men's leader by his female counterpart – along
with the tears that then supposedly stream down his face (lines 1031–4):

Women's Chorus Leader   Zeus above, what a great beast of a
gnat I see you've got in there! (*She pulls it out and shows it to
him.*) Take a look! . . .

Men's Leader   You've done me a real kindness, by Zeus. It'd been drilling wells into my eye for ages, so now it's been taken out tears are simply pouring down my face.

Of course, the advantage to us as modern readers of a play that was composed for the kind of large-scale theatre enjoyed by Athenians of the fifth century BCE is that many details of staging, clothing and comic business that might otherwise have been lost are preserved for us in Aristophanes' text.

The Action of the Play

(a) Introduction

This chapter aims to provide a walk-through of *Lysistrata* from its
hushed beginning, when a solitary, female figure paces up and down
in front of the spectators, to the rowdy, mass festivities of its ending.
Just as the various members of a modern audience bring different
perspectives to a performance of *Lysistrata*, so would those attending
the first production of the play on a late winter's day in 411 BCE have
brought a whole range of different expectations to the theatre. A select
few might have been involved in the rehearsals of *Lysistrata* or have
heard rumours about its subject matter – perhaps from cast members
or from the playwright himself. More Athenians still would have been
familiar with Aristophanes and his plays from previous competitions.
Some, however, will have been watching comedy for the very first
time. In the following pages, we will consider what they would
have seen.

(b) Plotting for peace: The sex strike and sedition (1–253)

The prologue of an ancient comedy is where so much of the magic
has to happen. In a theatrical tradition where there are no theatre
curtains or stage lighting to signal the start of the performance, and
where several thousand spectators – some perhaps sitting as far as
100 metres from the action – are crowded into an open-air auditorium,

a playwright like Aristophanes must use the opening scene of a play
not only to introduce major characters and themes, but also to settle
his audience down by seizing their interest and engaging them in the
action. Earlier surviving plays by Aristophanes often contain a
monologue either at the beginning or early on in the prologue which
lays out an intriguing situation from which the plot of the play then
proceeds. Examples include a father enumerating the problems his
spendthrift son has caused him (*Clouds*), the confinement of an
old man to the house by his son (*Wasps*) and a giant dung beetle being
fed by two weary slaves (*Peace*). Sometimes this monologue is
preceded – as in the last two plays mentioned – by a knockabout
'warm-up' routine, too, where two characters engage in jokey banter
both with each other and with the audience. But in *Lysistrata*, the
problem that is troubling the play's heroine (the war) and the great
idea she has for solving it (the sex strike and seizure of the Acropolis)
are articulated in a very different way. After emerging from the double
doors of the *skēnē* and briefly expressing her frustration about women,
Lysistrata is joined by her neighbour Calonice (line 6), whom she
then engages in conversation. After this exchange, and in a way that
conveniently allows the discussion both to develop and expand, a
whole host of women arrive almost simultaneously, first from various
parts of Attica (line 65) – including Myrrhine – and soon after from
other Greek states, too (line 78). In short, Aristophanes has conceived
the prologue in such a way as to allow Lysistrata to articulate her
concerns and plans gradually, without recourse to a lengthy exposition
or a direct address to the audience. Compared with Aristophanes'
other surviving plays, then, the prologue of *Lysistrata* is strikingly self-
contained, with the plot emerging in a far more organic way.

For those watching the original play in 411 BCE, one arresting
feature of the prologue may well have been its use of citizen women as
the main characters – this was perhaps a first for Old Comedy (see
Chapter 1 Section A). Instructively, Aristophanes seems to be at pains

early on in the play to underline the fact that these are 'ordinary', contemporary Athenian women. Lysistrata's familiarity with the religious events that she evokes at the beginning of the play (festivities connected with Bacchus, Pan and Genetyllis: lines 1–3), the early reference to Calonice as Lysistrata's 'neighbour' (at line 6) and the domestic detail provided by Calonice ('It's difficult for women to get out of the house, I tell you . . .', lines 16–19) would all have served to underline that these characters were not the kind of mythical women or fantasy figures that Old Comic audiences had seen before, but everyday citizen wives. Importantly, too, for how the original audience might have viewed the opening of the play, the appearance of two female characters outside the stage building would no doubt have evoked similar scenes at the beginning of tragedies like Sophocles' *Antigone*, where a conspiratorial meeting between women beyond the palace walls is a symptom of female discontent with the male ruler within (in the case of *Antigone*, at issue is the decision by Creon, the King of Thebes, not to allow the burial of the body of Antigone's brother, Polyneices, because of his treachery towards the city). Of course, a secret plot in response to dissatisfaction with male rule is a central element in *Lysistrata*, too – but whereas spectators of Sophocles' play could use their knowledge of myth to anticipate what Antigone and her sister would discuss out of men's earshot, Aristophanes has the opportunity to rouse genuine curiosity among the members of his audience about the nature of the (ultimately far larger) meeting that Lysistrata has called.

It is fascinating to trace the way in which Aristophanes builds suspense and tantalizes his audience in the prologue. One technique he uses here is constantly to stress the importance of Lysistrata's plan. Just in the first few lines, for example, we learn that the matter she wishes to discuss is 'big' and 'meaty' and that 'the salvation of all Greece' depends on her scheme (lines 23–4 and 29–30). The initial non-arrival of the women is a further technique used to build tension.

It allows Aristophanes to show how important the plan is to
Lysistrata by having her grow annoyed, whilst also signalling how
significant its announcement is to the other women, too, by having
them turn up from far and wide: first from far flung places in
Attica, then from hostile city-states such as Boeotia, Corinth and,
of course, Sparta, which is represented by the vigorous and straight-
talking Lampito. Later in the scene the women are also invited
to say how much Lysistrata's objective – 'bringing the war to an
end' (112) – would mean to them, thus raising the stakes higher still
(115–18):

> **Myrhine**   I think I'd even fillet myself and donate half my body
> – like a flatfish!
>
> **Lampito**   And I'd even climb to the top of Mount Taygetus, if I
> could get a glimpse of peace from there.

The apparent importance of Lysistrata's plan makes it intriguing
enough, but the fact that its revelation is put off until all the women
are present also builds suspense (Lysistrata holds back at 74–5, for
example: 'No, by Zeus, let's wait a bit more; it won't be long now . . .').
Similarly designed to rouse the audience's curiosity are the small
indications given about what the plan will comprise. We are told, for
example, that Greece's salvation is 'in the hands of its women' (30) and
will involve the use of sexy gowns, see-through shifts and erotic
footwear (46–8). Various physical attributes of women are mentioned
in the dialogue, too – such as Lampito's breasts and the Corinthian
woman's depilated genitalia (83 and 86–92) – adding a further splash
of risqué sexuality to the proceedings. In this way, the titillation and
tension neatly build to an explosive climax when the sex strike plan is
finally revealed at lines 119–24 of the play.

> **Lysistrata**   I will say it: for there's no reason to keep what I have
> to say a secret. Women, if we are going to compel the men to live
> at peace, we must refrain –

Calonice   From what? Tell us.

Lysistrata   You'll do it, then?

Calonice   We'll do it, even if it means death for us.

Lysistrata   Well then ... we must refrain from – cock!

Some of the features noted above are in evidence once more in this brief exchange: the importance of the plan is emphasized again and its revelation put off one last time. It is also worthy of note that, for all the sexual innuendoes (24–5; 59–60), the titillating details about women's dress and bodies (including the prodding of Lampito's 'tits': 83) – and even the mention of dildos (*olisboi*, 109) – that *peos*, 'cock', is the first obscenity uttered in the play: something that gives Lysistrata's announcement additional punch. Playfully, Aristophanes then throws this obscenity into stark relief by the use of high-flown, tragic-style language in Lysistrata's questions to the women as they recoil in horror (and ostensibly grow pale and cry) at the idea of giving up sex: 'What doth this pallor portend? Why floweth this stream of tears?' (127).

Along with the humour, playfulness and careful introduction of the plot and characters, the prologue also succeeds in introducing a number of themes that will prove important for the play as a whole. Stereotypes about younger women are seamlessly established, for example, such as their frivolity (women fail to arrive at the meeting on time to discuss 'a far from trivial matter', 14), their fondness for drink (during the oath-swearing scene, the women fight to be the first to drink and comment approvingly on the wine's colour and sweet smell, 206–7) and, crucially, their supposed love of sex, as exemplified by the negative reaction Lysistrata initially receives to her proposal ('Let the war carry on!' 'Anything, anything else ... rather than cock! There's *nothing* like it, Lysistrata dear!', 129–30, 133–5). Misogynistic attitudes are also given voice. We hear that men consider women to be 'utterly wicked' (*panourgoi*, 12), for instance, as well as 'vile' (*miarai*, 253).

Further important qualities of women are also established by Aristophanes in this scene. In addition to being sex-obsessed (which makes the whole concept of a female sex strike such rich fodder for a comedy, of course), the younger wives must also be endowed with sex appeal – enough to make it plausible that the men of Greece would be sufficiently inflamed with desire to put an end to the war. In a tradition that can be traced back to Homer, the chief weapon at the women's disposal is clothing (in her 'arming scene' in *Iliad* 14, Hera briefly diverts Zeus' attention away from the fighting at Troy by dressing in her sexiest attire in order to seduce him). The list of alluring garments mentioned by Lysistrata and the wives includes saffron gowns, see-through shifts, plus riverboat slippers and Persian shoes (43–53, 149–50, 219–20, 229–30), with the sexiness of these outfits further enhanced by make-up (44, 48) and by the depilation of their pubic hair (plucking into a neat triangle – the shape of the Greek letter 'delta' – is alluded to at line 151).[1] The extent to which citizen wives in classical Athens would have habitually owned such sexy garments is impossible to know, however. In her discussion of the play, Sarah Culpepper Stroup suggests that *Lysistrata*'s wives are portrayed as encroaching on the world of *hetairai*, i.e. 'prostitutes' or 'courtesans' – a category of women not specifically mentioned in the play (hardly surprisingly, since the plot relies on marital sex being the sole outlet for men's sexual desire). If the wives of Aristophanes are to be seen in this light, is their ownership of alluring clothing also an indication that they are straying into prostitutes' territory? Laura McClure thinks not, arguing in her article 'Courtesans Reconsidered' that the ownership and wearing of seductive apparel – albeit in private – was not uncommon for married women: for an Athenian wife, she suggests, such items were 'readily available and not out of the ordinary.'[2]

Alongside references to seductive clothing and physical allure, Aristophanes is also careful to establish less sexy elements of the women's domestic life. Indeed, the crowd assembled by Lysistrata consists of busy wives whose reasons for coming late to the meeting, Calonice suggests, might include attending to their husbands, overseeing the activities of domestic slaves and caring for babies (15–19). Later in the play, it is women's status as mothers – and for some younger women, their missed opportunity to become wives and mothers at all – that makes the current war so devastating (588–97). The women also miss their husbands (99–106) whose absence from home has disrupted the household (*oikos*) – and is set to disrupt the city (*polis*), too, once the women combine forces to pursue Lysistrata's plan. Order will ultimately be re-established at the end of the play, however, when the war is ended and women return home to assume the kind of sexual and domestic roles evoked in the prologue: that is, as desirable lovers and loyal wives and mothers.

Once the wives finally agree to the sex strike plan (line 167), the focus swiftly shifts to the swearing of an oath of chastity and allegiance – an idea suggested by Lysistrata at lines 181–2: 'Why don't we join together in swearing an oath as quickly as possible, so as to make our pact unbreakable?' The ensuing action provides some memorable comic highlights with women's stereotypical fondness for both wine and sex deftly exploited. The women are particularly excited by the giant vessels that the enslaved Scythian woman brings out for drinking, for example – presumably a larger-than-life drinking bowl and (possibly phallic?) wine-jar ('My dearest ladies, what enormous pottery!' 200). When it comes to sex, too, Lysistrata and Calonice seem intriguingly familiar with the playfully named 'lioness on a cheese-grater' position (231–2).[3] But as well as providing a rich mix of visual and verbal humour, this scene also shows the wives starting to negotiate their new roles as women undertaking public activities that are traditionally the preserve of men – in this case, the swearing of oaths. Lysistrata's initial proposal is to seal their pact with a sacrifice, 'by slaughtering a beast ... over a shield' (188–9), but when this is questioned by Calonice, Lysistrata concedes that a shield is hardly appropriate for an oath about peace (189–97) – something that might equally be said about bloodshed. Unusually, then, Lysistrata changes her approach and proposes instead an oath sworn over a jar of wine, an idea that brilliantly combines women's supposed fondness for drink with the tradition of pouring libations of wine to confirm a peace treaty. Yet when the wine jar is eventually opened by Lysistrata it is nevertheless described as a 'sacrifice' (*sphagia*: 204), whose 'blood gushes out well' (205). There is, then, a sense here of the women appropriating a traditionally male role (blood sacrifice), but imaginatively reconfiguring it in an inventive and appropriately feminine way (since it avoids bloodshed whilst also allowing the women to indulge their supposed love of drinking).[4] Importantly, too, in overseeing this 'sacrifice', Lysistrata is cast as something of a priestess figure: a role she arguably assumes elsewhere in the play as well (see Chapter 3 Section A for discussion of the possible correspondences between the fictional Lysistrata and the real-life Priestess of Athena Polias in classical Athens named Lysimache).

With discussion of the sex strike dominating the opening of *Lysistrata*, the other key element of Lysistrata's plan – the women's occupation of the Acropolis, which will underpin the action of the play for the next 500 lines – receives only scant attention. It is not until lines 176–9 that it is briefly announced by Lysistrata ('We're going to seize the Acropolis today; the older women have been assigned that duty'). Later, an off-stage cry signals that this has been successfully accomplished (240–2):

Lampito   What was that shout for?

Lysistrata   It's just what I was telling you about: the women have now captured the citadel of the goddess.

A number of things happen very quickly at this point in the play. For example, Lysistrata sends Lampito back to Sparta to arrange things there – thus identifying Sparta as the other key player alongside Athens in the peace process – whilst also pronouncing that the other non-Athenian women should be left in Athens as hostages (*homēroi*). Lysistrata also instructs the Athenian wives to go inside the Acropolis and 'help the other women . . . to bar the doors' (245–6). Logically, this all makes little sense. For a start, the sex strike was previously envisaged as relying on the wives sitting enticingly at home, dressed to impress, not shut inside the Acropolis in the clothes they arrived in. And how are the women from Corinth and Boeotia supposed to organize sex strikes in their respective cities if they are being held captive in Athens? How, too, are the men of Athens even meant to learn about the sex strike? It is alluded to only obliquely in the following scenes before it re-emerges as a major part of the plot at line 705. Logical consistency is clearly not Aristophanes' concern here. His aim is rather to drive the action forward – something that he skilfully does without giving his audience too much time to think about the flaws in his plot. With Lysistrata's instructions to the younger Athenian women to join their older counterparts, the scene is also instantaneously transformed from an anonymous street to the entrance to the Acropolis, with the stage doors now to be imagined as the gates leading to the Athenian citadel.[5] As the women close these gates behind them, the barred doors might be said neatly to combine the play's two plotlines. As various scholars have noted, they stand as an emblem not only of the women's occupation of the Acropolis but arguably of the sex strike, too, since they symbolically mirror the way in which the entrances to women's bodies are now closed to their husbands.[6]

(c) Fire and water: The choruses collide (254–386)

The parodos, or choral entry song, represents the point at which an Old Comic poet introduces his audience to the play's chorus – often with a flourish, as in Aristophanes' *Acharnians*, where the twenty-four chorus members (*choreutai*) rush onstage in hostile pursuit of the comedy's protagonist, or in his *Birds* where they get to show off their spectacular, individualized costumes for the first time. Rather than experiencing a dazzling moment of energetic revelation, however, the original audience of *Lysistrata* is left gradually to realize that the old men ambling into view at line 254 of the play, weighed down by logs, torches and coals, are just twelve in number. The audience must wait until line 319 to learn the identity of the second semi-chorus – a group of old women, it transpires – who arrive somewhat more energetically on the scene, armed with pitchers of water.

The old men are deftly characterized in the parodos through both their actions and words. As they make their slow progress towards the doors of the *skēnē*, their age is first alluded to ('A long life contains so very many surprises!', 256) and then underscored by their recollections of past glories which associate them with the glory days not only of the Persian Wars (285) but even the final years of Athens' tyranny over a century before (274–82: see Chapter 1 Section D). Their misogyny is also made fully apparent (lines 260–1, 283) as, in time, is their preparedness to use violence against the old women with whom they become locked in conflict ('I'll beat you and gut you clean out of that old skin of yours!', 364).

Just as the men's aim of 'setting ablaze all the women who have undertaken and pursued this enterprise [i.e. occupying the Acropolis]' (268–9), neatly provides Aristophanes with a pretext to have this ageing crew march onstage as a group, the arrival of the women's chorus is also achieved in a dramatically plausible way: they come 'bringing water to save [their] fellow citizens (*dēmotis*) from being burnt' (333–5). The old women soon show themselves to be more than a match for the old men in their verbal and physical ferocity: they call them 'wickedly wicked' and 'stupid old men' (350, 336) and offer gloriously vicious ripostes to their threats ('I'll sink my teeth into you and tear out your guts and lungs!' 367). However, the two groups are nevertheless united in their piety towards Athena and respect of her sacred citadel. The men's mission is articulated as an attempt to help and defend the goddess (303–4), whose sanctuary they describe as '*my* Acropolis' (263), and they even address Athena directly as Lady Victory (*despoina Nikē*, 317) – perhaps turning at this point piously to acknowledge the Temple of Athena Nike which stood close to the gates of the Acropolis, overlooking the Theatre of Dionysus. The women pray directly to Athena, too, evoking her as the city's

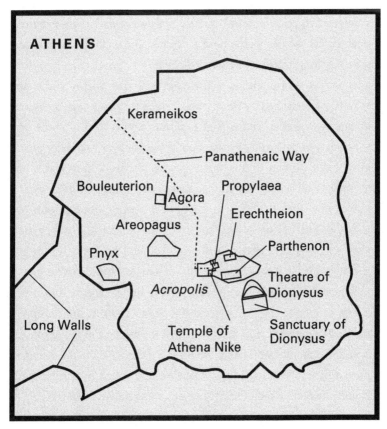

Map 2.1 The city of Athens in the late fifth century BCE.

'golden-crested guardian' and calling on her to be their ally by bringing water if any man should set her sanctuary on fire (344–50).

Wood, fire and water are symbols expertly exploited by Aristophanes in the parodos to add to the characterization of these two groups. The old men find carrying the wood challenging, for example, and when lighting the fire they temporarily blind themselves with the smoke (295 and 305). The old women on the other hand encounter no such difficulties with their pitchers, which they nimbly manoeuvre to drench the men with water (381–4). Put simply, the women outwit the men with their superior speed and organization. Noteworthy, too, is the way in which the verbal pyrotechnics and slapstick involved in the exchange of threats, the old men's haplessness and their eventual drenching by the old women are all capable of making the parodos one of the humorous highlights of the play.

Arguably, the importance of these symbols – wood, fire and water – is not just restricted to the parodos, since they can also be linked thematically to other elements of *Lysistrata*'s plot. The old men's fire, for instance, mirrors the fiery passion of the younger men later in the play. The old women in their turn are easily able to quench this fire with their water when they choose, just as the younger women would be able, whenever *they* choose, to quench their husbands' passion. There is also sexual symbolism to be found in the phallic logs carried by the men, which contrast with the women's pitchers (which are plausibly 'yonic', that is to say, evocative of female reproductive organs). Further sexual imagery can also be found in the men's attempts to use the logs as a battering ram against the closed gates of the Acropolis (308–9). In a different vein, fire also recalls the burning of the Acropolis (including the ancient Temple of Athena Polias) when the Persians sacked Athens in 480 BCE, just as wood and water in combination recall the navy on which the city's power was historically based.[7]

A particularly thought-provoking reading of the parodos – and its use of wood, fire and water as symbols by Aristophanes – has been proposed by Christopher Faraone, who considers the specific imagery of women appearing with pitchers to put out a fire.[8] As he highlights, there are parallels between the events of *Lysistrata*'s parodos and certain 'salvation myths' – with which fifth-century BCE theatre audiences would been familiar from tragedies such as Euripides' lost *Alcmene* – where helpless female figures (like Alcmene) are rescued from being burnt alive while seeking sanctuary at an altar. Judged against this mythical model, the old women with their pitchers are cast in a positive light as saviours and supporters of an underdog, whereas the old men are cast in the role of cruel aggressors. Faraone also explores the significance of a further mythical paradigm which sees a heroic male figure threatened with being burnt on a pyre only to be rescued and reborn: there is a tradition of Heracles suffering this fate, for example (who is tellingly evoked at line 296). Important for Faraone's argument is that the women of *Lysistrata* do not put out the men's fire with their water, but rather pour it over the old men themselves – with the dousing then referred to as a 'wedding bath' (a ritual conceived of as promoting fertility in a bridegroom) and something that will make them 'sprout' afresh (377, 384). In this way, he argues, the old women are subtly presented as the saviours of the old men, with the water they use to soak them holding the promise of reinvigoration and rejuvenation. Chiming neatly with Faraone's argument is a fact often noted by scholars that the women of *Lysistrata* make repeated claims that they will 'save' the city of Athens and its menfolk.[9]

(d) Women on top: The Magistrate scene (387–614)

The first male character we meet in the play besides the semi-chorus of old men is an ally of theirs, the Magistrate or Proboulos, who arrives in the company of a number of Scythian archers (these were public slaves who performed a police-like function in classical Athens and whose distinctive dress would have immediately signalled their identity to the audience: see Figure 2.1). The Probouloi were relative newcomers to the civic life of Athens, a board of ten 'older men' originally appointed in the aftermath of the Sicilian Disaster with powers to take swift action on the city's behalf in response to emergencies (Thucydides 8.1.3–4: see Chapter 1 Section B).[10] In this capacity – and as someone who deals with the purchase of timber to equip warships and therefore requires access to state funds stored on the Acropolis (421–3) – the Proboulos represents a particularly fitting male authority figure for Lysistrata and her followers to spar with. Aristophanes characterizes him as ignorant of the women's motives

Figure 2.1 Athenian red-figure plate depicting an (unbearded) archer in Scythian costume, painted by Epiktetos, *c.* 520–510 BCE.

for occupying the Acropolis, thereby providing a convenient pretext for Lysistrata to articulate her grievances and the rationale behind her plan.

Throughout the scene, the Magistrate displays similar misogynistic views to the old men, but also introduces some new perspectives on male–female relations into the play. In his opening remarks, for instance, he ascribes the women's seizure of the Acropolis to 'female decadence' (*truphē*, 387), but the example of self-indulgent behaviour to which he then compares the women's actions subtly exposes the dangers inherent in men being unable to look beyond their misogynistic prejudices. The Magistrate relates how a speech in support of the Sicilian Expedition in the Athenian Assembly a few years before was interrupted by a woman celebrating a domestic religious festival nearby (the Adonia), crying 'Alas, Adonis!' and 'Grieve for Adonis!' (393 and 396). Since the beautiful young Adonis of myth was gored to death by a boar, it would be possible in hindsight to see the woman's cries as a prophetic warning about the untimely death in Sicily of men in their prime, of course, and as an example of how men ignore women at their peril. However, the Proboulos fails to ascribe any significance to this female intervention in men's affairs: rather, he simply offers it up as an example of women's 'depraved activities' (398).

The Magistrate continues on his theme of female depravity with a set of anecdotes that betray a similarly blinkered view of women. He complains that men 'assist their wives in their depravity and teach them to be decadent' (*truphan*, 404–5) by their unwitting use of *double entendre*s (407–13):

> in craftsmen's shops we say things like this: 'Goldsmith, that necklace you repaired – my wife was dancing one evening and the pin's fallen out of the hole. Now, I've got to sail over to Salamis; but if you're free, could you come over in the evening and, using all your expertise, fit a pin in her hole?'

As well as injecting some blatantly smutty humour into this scene, these anecdotes serve to underline once again how men's words can result in damaging actions (a speech in the Assembly can encourage the pursuit of a disastrous military campaign; a careless conversation can encourage adultery). But they also reveal a world view which credits women with limited insight or agency: a woman's cries are to be written off, however prophetic they turn out to be, and extra-marital sex is presented as something that happens as a result of a conversation between two men rather than, say, something a woman might actively invite or pursue herself (or, indeed, reject).

The notion that women have limited capacity for independent action and are not worth listening to is very much held up to scrutiny later in this scene, when Lysistrata finally comes to explain her plan and rationale. But first the Magistrate makes a further mistaken assumption about women, namely that he will be able to put them in their place with threats and violence. Just as the old women got the better of the old men in the parodos, however, so do Lysistrata's comrades show themselves to be more than a match for the Proboulos and his Scythian Archers. Far from being intimidated, the women prove themselves capable of both talking tough ('if you come near her, I'll yank out your well-anchored hair till you scream!', 447-8) and fighting in an organized and effective way. It is only when the men's violence fails that the Proboulos engages in dialogue with Lysistrata, prompted by the leader of the chorus of old men to find out 'for what reason [women] have occupied the great rock of the forbidden Acropolis' (481-2).

Initially, the motives behind the occupation are concisely outlined by Lysistrata, 'to keep the money safe and stop [men] from waging war because of it' (488), since it is money, she alleges, that motivates corrupt politicians to stir up trouble (489-91).[11] Subsequently, however, she goes on to articulate at some length her vision for how women might effectively run the city, as well as her complaints against men and their management of public affairs. As for what a future Athens ruled by women might look like, she suggests that skills traditionally practised by women in the household – such as the management of domestic finances – might be applied to the city at large (see Chapter 1 Section D). Particularly striking is the extended wool-working simile-cum-metaphor that she uses to explain how the city's problems can be solved (567–86). When asked by the Magistrate how she will unravel the large confusion that currently exists in international affairs, she says (568–70):

> It's just like when we've got a skein of wool that's all tangled. We take it like this, carefully drawing it apart with spindles, first this way, then that. And this is just how we will disentangle this war, too, if you'll let us: we'll sort it out by sending embassies first this way, then that.

As her speech continues, she talks about washing, beating, carding and weaving the wool, with each of these steps made analogous to an action that the city should take. The result of these actions, in the words of Lysistrata's metaphor, is that the women will be able to 'weave a nice warm cloak (*chlaina*) for the people to wear' (586). There is a homeliness in this image as well as a beguiling logic in the idea that the city can be run like a household – ridiculous as the notion of female rule would no doubt have seemed to a contemporary, predominantly male Athenian audience. But contained within Lysistrata's metaphor are also some radical ideas for expanding Athens' citizen body as well as some violent imagery ('you have to ... bash out the villains with a rod ... card out [conspirators] and pluck off their heads', 576–8: for further discussion, see Chapter 3 Section C).

When it comes to articulating their complaints, the women make a number of points about the disruption and destructiveness of war in this scene, ranging from the way in which it distorts everyday life (men doing their shopping in armour; husbands absent on campaign:

555–64, 591–2) to the devastating poignancy of women losing their sons in battle or – in the case of very young women – being deprived of the opportunity to marry (588–90, 594–97).[12] When it comes to male–female relations, however, one of the chief complaints that Lysistrata harks back to is the notion of men's poor decision making and their unpreparedness to listen to women. She describes scenarios in which a husband refuses to discuss with his wife what was resolved at Athens' Assembly and even threatens her with violence when she seeks to offer him advice about public policy (507–22).

Women may have been forced into silence previously, but towards the end of this scene it is Lysistrata and the women who silence the Proboulos, symbolically feminizing him by dressing him in female accoutrements (532–7), and compelling him to listen to them ('Be quiet!' 529 and 534). Once more, then, the women prove themselves capable of being active agents and demonstrate that they have substantial and thought-provoking contributions to make to civic discourse. Noteworthy, too, is that the theme of male salvation is once again prominent in this scene, with particular emphasis given to the positive interventions of which women are capable (see Section C above). Lysistrata repeatedly uses the different forms of the verb 'to save' (*sōizō*), telling the Proboulos that women 'will save' Athens' menfolk (498) and that she will actively compel him 'to be saved' whether he likes it or not (*sōsomen, sōthēsei, sōsteon*, 498–501). To drive the point home, at the end of the episode his need for salvation is visually underscored by being dressed by the women as a corpse (599–613).

(e) Pride and pathos: A choral stand-off (615–705)

Following the departure of the Magistrate and his slaves, Lysistrata and her companions return to the Acropolis through the double doors of the *skēnē*, leaving the two semi-choruses alone in the *orchēstra*. At this point, the original spectators might reasonably have expected a parabasis (lit. a 'going forward' or 'stepping forward'). This is a structured set of metrically diverse songs, normally found in the middle of an Old Comic play, during which the chorus members move towards the audience and divest themselves of their outer garments before offering various opinions and advice – ostensibly speaking either in character or on behalf of the playwright. Rather than a formal parabasis, however, what we find in *Lysistrata* is an exchange between the two semi-choruses and their respective chorus leaders (*koryphaioi*): a mixture of song and speech, consisting of four blocks in total. First the men's chorus leader speaks (614–5 and 626–35) and the old men sing (616–25), then the women's chorus leader speaks (636–7 and 648–57) and the old women sing (638–47), and following this the whole formula is effectively repeated in lines 658–705 (this form of exchange follows the tradition of paired lyric stanzas traditionally found at the end of a parabasis, known as an epirrhematic syzygy). The semi-chorus of old women address the audience directly ('Here we begin, all you citizens . . ', 638), with the spirit of the parabasis also apparent from details such as the women offering the city advice (638–9, 648) and the removal of clothes. Initially, the two semi-choruses, first the old men and then the old women, take off their outer clothing (615 and 637) – but then, unusually, their remaining attire, too (661–2 and 686–7), leaving them all 'stage naked' (see Chapter 1 Section E and Figure 1.2).[13]

Many of the themes of previous scenes are revisited and extended in these songs. The women invoke their status as mothers contributing sons to the city (651) and also allege that men misuse public funds and pass bad decrees in the Assembly (652–3 and 703–4). The men complain about the women's attempts to offer advice (626) and fail to acknowledge their capacity for independent action (suspecting instead that the women have been 'stirred up' in an attempt to establish a pro-Spartan dictatorship: 619–25). The association of women with

animals – something of a leitmotif in the play – recurs here, too (while
men use 'animal' as a misogynistic insult at 468, the women habitually
claim their animality as a positive feature: at 684, they compare
themselves to a 'sow', just as they have previously likened themselves
to a 'bitch' at line 363 and 'wasp' at 475).[14] The theme of male
revitalization and rebirth is repeated, too, given more than a hint of
pathos by the leader of the chorus of old men with his earnest appeal
to his elderly comrades to regain their youthful vigour: 'now, *now* we
must become young again, let our whole bodies take flight and shake
off this old skin of ours' (669–70).

Something that links the old men and women is the pride with
which they both recollect the services they performed for the city in
their youth. For their part, the men allude once more to the Persian
Wars and the role they played in end of Athens' dictatorship (674–5 and
664–5). But it is the women who dwell with particular pride on their
youthful achievements, recalling the roles they played as girls in civic
religion in service of Athena and other goddesses (641–7; the activity of
weaving is also evoked here in the women's claim to have been
Arrephoroi, young girls of noble families who helped to weave Athena's
sacred robe (*peplos*) ahead of the annual Panathenaea procession). The
antipathy between the two semi-choruses is also vibrantly reinforced at
the end of each block of song and speech by a specific threat of violence:
'I'll smack you in the jaw with this boot,' say the women at 657, for
example, to which the men later retort, 'We should grab them all by this
neck of theirs and fasten it in the stocks' (680–1).

(f) The women waver: The strike plot and choral debate (706–828)

As the semi-choruses finish sparring, Lysistrata emerges from the
Acropolis and, as she informs us, paces around 'to and fro in despair'

(709), possibly in such a way as to recall the opening of the play. The brief exchange she then has with the leader of the chorus of old women is peppered with high-flown elements borrowed from tragedy, including vocabulary (e.g. *anassa*, 'sovereign queen', 706; *domoi*, 'palace', 707), phraseology (e.g. 'it is shameful to say, yet grievous to remain silent', 713) and the use of literary devices such as repetition ('What say you? What say you?', 'The truth! The truth!', 710–11). This lofty tone is soon punctured, however, when Lysistrata finally reveals the source of the women's troubles: 'To summarize our tale: we need a *fuck!*' (*binētiōmen*, 715).

This blunt declaration marks a shift in focus back to the sex strike (which has only been alluded to briefly since the prologue, namely at 525–6, 551–4 and 696–7). Time has evidently passed and Lysistrata now relates how the women are 'running away all over the place' (719) and 'coming out with all manner of excuses to go back home' (726–7). The scene is now set for her to encounter a series of women attempting to escape from the Acropolis, each with a thinly veiled excuse as to her motives – although, somewhat atypically for Old Comedy, the illicit sex that these women are seeking is with their own husbands rather than a lover. The First Woman wants to tend to her fleeces by 'spreading them on the bed' (728–34), while the Second Women wants to 'peel' flax (which evokes the image of the foreskin of an erect penis being retracted, 735–41). Notable here are not just the clever word play and humorous exploitation of women's stereotypical love of sex, but also that the excuses offered involve female chores traditionally undertaken in the home (and cloth-working at that, which relates to the play's weaving imagery). There is arguably a suggestion here that if the women cave in now, they might, as John Vaio puts it, simply 'return to domestic servitude in a world badly mismanaged by men'.[15] The Third Woman who tries to escape feigns pregnancy, still persisting in her story when Lysistrata discovers that her oversized belly is in fact the 'sacred helmet' of Athena (751–2). Her allegedly 'male' baby (748) turns out to be a piece of armour, recalling once more the idea of women as mothers of sons who serve as soldiers. Some scholars have also seen the 'birth' of a military helmet at a time when reproductive, marital sex is no longer taking place as evoking the notion of the sterility of war.[16]

A notable feature of this scene is the way in which Aristophanes invokes a sense of the materiality of the Acropolis as a religious space. In particular, there are mentions of statues and animals connected with Athena, which in turn serve to remind the audience of the different guises under which the goddess was worshipped in her sacred precinct. For example, the 'sacred helmet' used by the Third Women to feign her pregnancy is probably to be envisaged as the helmet belonging to one of the statues of Athena that stood on the Acropolis, such as the 9-metre-high (30 feet) bronze statue of Athena Promachos ('Athena who fights in front') which stood on the Acropolis, towering over the city. A few lines later there is a reference to the Acropolis' 'guardian serpent' (759), a sculpted version of which could be found curled up under the shield of the famous gold and ivory statue of Athena Parthenos ('Athena the virgin') which stood in the Parthenon itself (see Figure 2.2).[17] And at line 760, there is mention of the Acropolis owls which were sacred to Athena in her role as Athena Polias ('Athena, guardian of the city').[18] Fighter, virgin and guardian of Athens are, of course, particularly appropriate roles of Athena to evoke, since they neatly align with the current preoccupations of Lysistrata and her sex-striking comrades.

The escapee sequence is finally rounded off by Lysistrata's production of an oracle (line 767) – a tool of political persuasion in classical Athens that is regularly mocked in Aristophanes' plays – which bluntly prophesies success for the women if they adhere to the sex strike (770-6).[19] As Lysistrata and the others return to the Acropolis, the two semi-choruses then deliver a further pair of competitive songs accompanied by yet more insults and threats of

Figure 2.2 The Varvakeion Athena, *c.* 200–250 CE, a copy of the statue of Athena Parthenos by Pheidias which stood in the Parthenon.

violence. In the first ode, the old men tell the story of a man called Melanion, who fled from marriage and settled in a mountain wilderness 'because of his hatred' of women (793). In reply, the old women relate the tale of Timon, a wanderer who was supposedly friendly to women but 'whose countenance was hemmed round with impassable thorns', in his case 'because of his hatred' of men (809–11 and 813). While concisely conveying the lengths to which their loathing of the opposite sex drove these two men, these songs might also be said to lay the foundations for the reconciliation that is to come between the old men and old women. After all, what these lyric passages illustrate are the negative consequences of such hatred: both Melanion and Timon cut themselves off from civilization and deny themselves the kind of domestic, married life to which the women – and ultimately the men – of *Lysistrata* seek to return.[20]

(g) The seduction scene: Cinesias and Myrrhine (829–953)

At the end of the choral interlude, the audience's attention is drawn to the roof of the *skēnē* where Lysistrata appears, quietly looking off into the distance, apparently surveying Athens from the walls of the Acropolis. She soon cries out, prompting other women to join her. What she has spotted is a man approaching, 'driven mad [and] overcome by the rites of Aphrodite' (831–2), who is subsequently identified by Myrrhine as her husband, Cinesias. This marks the point in the play – evidently six days after Lysistrata's campaign began (881) – where the focus shifts to the effects of the sex strike on the younger men of Athens. In another humorous highpoint in the play, Cinesias now comes into view complaining of his 'suffering' – and sporting an enormous erect phallus (845–6).

Aristophanes builds huge comic potential into this scene, making generous use throughout of physical and visual humour as well as risqué *double entendres*. Cinesias' requests for sex are met with prevarication on the part of Myrrhine, whose constant running back and forth for various objects, supposedly to assist their love-making – a bed, mattress, pillow, blanket and scent – is strung out into a long comic sequence. All the while Cinesias' frustration grows increasingly intense, with his desperation never more clearly expressed than when he shouts, 'I want to fuck!' (934). His oversized erection, which serves as such a potent symbol of the sex strike, is repeatedly used to underpin jokes in this scene, such as when Myrrhine offers him an alabastos, a type of perfume bottle whose length and cylindrical shape gave it phallic connotations, and he points to his erect penis saying, 'I've already got one!' (947; cf. 846–7, 861–2 and 937). Indeed, this string of hard-on gags can be traced all the way back to Lysistrata's initial encounter with Cinesias when she first engages him in conversation, claiming to be the 'daytime sentry' (847–9).

Lysistrata   Who is that *standing* within the sentry line?

Cinesias   It's me.

Lysistrata   A man?

Cinesias   (***signalling his erect phallus***) Too right, a man!

The sexual tone of this scene is further underscored by the couple's names. While Cinesias is a real, attested name in the classical era, it is nevertheless suggestive of the Greek verb *kineō*, which as well as signifying 'I move' also has the colloquial meaning 'I screw'. Reinforcing the sexual overtones of his name is Cinesias' claim to come from the Attic deme of Paionidai (852), which puns on the Greek verb *paiō*, meaning 'I strike, hit', or again colloquially, 'I bang, screw'. Myrrhine was evidently a common female name in classical Athens, but in a similar vein is evocative of *murta*, 'myrtle berries', a euphemism for female sexual organs.[21] That said, Myrrhine has a number of further resonances that are potentially significant for this play. It was the name of both the wife of Hippias, the last tyrant of Athens (Thucydides 6.55.1: see Chapter 1 Section C) and also of a Priestess of Athena Nike in the late fifth century BCE.[22]

A significant aspect of the Cinesias/Myrrhine episode is that it marks a departure in the way in which *Lysistrata*'s battle of the sexes theme is played out. As befits a seduction scene, there is a shift away from the kind of direct confrontation exhibited by the two semi-choruses or in Lysistrata's encounter with the Magistrate to a more nuanced tussle between husband and wife in which persuasive and erotic language come to the fore. It is still Lysistrata who continues to command the action, however; this time by orchestrating the encounter between Cinesias and Myrrhine. She also sets the tone for the seduction, teasingly addressing Cinesias in language dripping with sexual undertones (the egg and apple she mentions having phallic associations, since their shape and texture evoke the head of the penis; 853–7).

> Greetings, my dearest man! For your name is hardly unfamiliar among us nor is it without repute. Your wife always has you ... *on her lips.* Whenever she picks up an egg or an apple, she says, 'Let this be for Cinesias!'

Myrrhine's tactics in this scene are to tantalize Cinesias by alluding to her affection for him ('I won't say that I don't love you', 905), gradually removing her clothes (she takes off her breastband at 931 and shoes at 950), and making increasingly strong promises of sex. Indeed, her initial refusal to sleep with her husband (905) soon turns into an open declaration of her willingness to do so (935), yet the act itself is repeatedly put off by Myrrhine who brings onstage a series of accoutrements which comically pile up to create an outdoor public bedroom. All along she makes her bargaining position clear, however: sex comes at price, namely that men must 'reconcile their differences and stop the war' (900–1). Indeed, when she finally disappears through the *skēnē* door, leaving Cinesias aroused and unsatisfied, her final words to her husband are: 'Do make sure that you vote to make peace, my dearest' (951–2). Some scholars detect in this scene the characterization of Myrrhine as a *hetaira* (prostitute), driving a hard bargain for her services at the bidding of her brothel-keeper, Lysistrata.[23]

The way in which Cinesias is portrayed as engaging with his wife is also of interest. Although he is ultimately unsuccessful in his attempt to have sex, his persuasive tactics are clearly tailored to address female concerns – a far cry from the hostile misogyny that men have been meting out to women up to this point. Notably, Cinesias' use of the baby to lure his wife out of the Acropolis, appealing to her maternal nature ('Don't you pity your child …?', 880), and his reference to Myrrhine's 'weaving being carried off by the hens' (896–7) both correspond to topics that Lysistrata and her followers have repeatedly raised: that is, women's role as mothers and the importance of textiles and weaving. While Cinesias' actions are no doubt presented as cynical – he comically disposes of the baby in a cursory fashion, for example, as soon as it is expedient (908–9) – there is arguably an indication here of common ground: a shared understanding between the sexes of the significance of certain roles in which women take pride (see also Chapter 4 Section B on Cinesias' use of language in this scene). This might usefully be seen as part of a broader pattern of points of contact between men and women that are subtly articulated throughout the play, especially prominent in the case of the two semi-choruses who, as we have seen, both exhibit piety towards Athena, for example, and both voice their pride in the services they performed for the city in their youth. Of course, these points of commonality pave the way dramatically for the two sides' eventual reconciliation, helping to make it seem all the less forced.

(h) The men feel the tension (954–1014)

Following Myrrhine's departure, there is a brief exchange between Cinesias and the chorus of old men (composed in anapaests, a metre often used in tragedy for exchanges between a character and the chorus and probably delivered here as semi-sung, semi-spoken recitative). Cinesias is the first to speak, briefly lamenting his treatment at the hands of his wife and making his sexual desperation more than clear ('Alas, what am I to do? Who am I to fuck . . .?', 954). The leader of the chorus of old men then replies with a passage which, in a pattern characteristic of a number of Aristophanes' lyrics, begins with high-flown tragic language ('Truly it is by a terrible pain, o wretched one, that thou art worn down . .', 959) only to dip in tone ('What kidney could endure it? What soul? What *bollocks* . . .?', 962–3) before ending low, in this case with a primary obscenity ('. . . what crotch, what loins could stand being at high tension without an early-morning *fuck*?', 964–6).[24] Noteworthy throughout these rhythmical sequences is the medicalization of Cinesias' predicament. In addition to the chorus naming various body parts that have supposedly been affected by his enforced sexual abstinence – kidneys, bollocks, loins, crotch – Cinesias himself also complains of 'convulsions' (*antispasmos*, 967), thereby extending his previous use of medical terms to describe the effects of his permanently ithyphallic state: he earlier refers to 'cramps' and 'spasms' (*spasmos* and *tetanos*, 845–6). As Natalia Tsoumpra points out, earlier in the play 'it was the women who were shown to suffer from lack of sex; now, it is the men's turn to suffer accordingly'.[25] The exchange ends with a further short passage in which Cinesias wishes for a whirlwind sent by Zeus to sweep up his wife and bring her down on his 'rock-hard dick' (*psōle*, 979) – a crude fantasy that once more serves to underline his desperation and inability to find sexual relief.[26]

Following these songs comes a short episode simply brimming with sexual humour in which a Spartan Herald encounters an Athenian – who is probably Cinesias (though some scholars prefer to imagine Cinesias departing and an unnamed Athenian arriving).[27] At first, the jokes revolve around the Spartan's struggles to hide his erect phallus which culminate in an implausible explanation of what he is hiding inside his cloak when he claims that the protrusion is 'a Spartan message staff' (*skutala*, 991: a kind of stick around which messages written on leather were wound).[28] Once his erection is revealed, however, there comes a further wave of jokes based on *double entendres*, ranging from a lewd reference to women's sexual organs as 'pork-bags' (1001) to the playful description by the Spartan of how matters are at home (995–6): 'All Sparta has *risen up* and all our allies have *stiffened* their resolve . . .'[29]

Dramatically, this brief encounter serves the important purpose of moving the plot quickly forwards. Cinesias is shown as coming to recognize that, rather than being confined to Athens, the sex strike is Panhellenic – a 'conspiracy by women everywhere' (1007). This in turn acts as a trigger for him and the Spartan Herald to depart in order to initiate the all-important business of assembling delegates from their respective cities to negotiate a peace settlement.

(i) Reconciliation (1014–1215)

The choral exchange that follows the departure of Cinesias and the Spartan Herald marks a significant turning point in the action. Throughout the play, the interaction between the two semi-choruses forms what Alan Sommerstein has poetically called 'a counterpoint to the main melody of the action', with the behaviour of the old men and old women often prefiguring that of the younger characters.[30] The parodos, for example, is the first glimpse we get of men and women in direct conflict. At this point in *Lysistrata*, the choruses anticipate the actions of the play's younger men and women once again, this time by being the first to reconcile their differences.

It is the old women who initiate this reconciliation. Their leader offers to be a 'firm friend' to the men's leader (*bebaion . . . philēn*, 1017) and, despite his initial hostility, she proceeds to care for him by tenderly clothing him and taking out a gnat that is in his eye. This action can be seen as symbolically restoring the men's sight, of course: now that they can see clearly, the men are content to call a truce and make peace (1040–1)!³¹ The two semi-choruses then unite to sing their first ode as one combined chorus, addressing the audience directly. In a brief aside, they acknowledge the fact that the spectators in the theatre might reasonably expect them to deliver some form of attack on a public figure and/or political commentary, as choruses in Old Comedy so often do (usually in the parabasis, but sometimes in a 'second parabasis', too, towards the end of a play). However, they use their direct address here simply to explain that their songs will be free of personal abuse, offering by way of explanation the fraught situation in which Athens currently finds itself (1043–9).

> We are not preparing,
> Gentlemen, to say a single nasty thing
> About any of the citizens,
>
> Quite the opposite:
> To say and do nothing but
> Good. For you've got quite enough
> Bad things on your plate as it is.

The choruses then proceed to deliver a matched pair of jaunty lyrics markedly different in tone from anything they have said or sung before – a formula that is later repeated at the end of the reconciliation scene (see below).

As the chorus falls silent, first a Spartan, then an Athenian delegation arrives. The fact that the men all sport erect phalluses allows for a further round of sexual jokes: the newly united chorus repeatedly mocks the new arrivals' state of arousal ('things seem to have got worse – terribly *inflamed!*' 1078–9), while the young men express their desperation and preparedness to make a peace settlement. Into this scene strides Lysistrata, who is greeted by the chorus in exulted terms as a supreme arbiter of the Greeks' disputes. Some scholars have seen in these lines and the qualities with which she is associated an identification between Lysistrata and Athena herself.

Sommerstein has even suggested that she might have been dressed to resemble Athena, perhaps wearing a garment reminiscent of the goddess' distinctive aegis (1108–11).[32]

> **Chorus**   Hail, most courageous (*andreiotatē*) of all women! Now you must prove yourself to be forceful and gentle, noble and ordinary, august and kindly, worldly-wise; for the leaders of the Greeks, overwhelmed by your charm (*iunx*), have come together and jointly entrusted all their complaints to your arbitration.

Lysistrata very much commands the action from this point on. One of her first deeds is to summon out of the Acropolis a naked young woman – the personification of Reconciliation (*Diallagē*) itself – who forms part of a long line of similarly sexually alluring female figures that appear in Aristophanic plays (other examples include Peace Treaties in *Acharnians* and Festival and Harvest in *Peace*).[33] How Reconciliation and other such women were portrayed in the original productions has been much discussed, but the scholarly consensus – which probably makes the most sense theatrically – is that they each would have been played by a male actor wearing appropriate padding (the other possibility that is sometimes suggested being a naked female slave).[34] In accordance with Lysistrata's instructions, Reconciliation helps to station the Athenian and Spartan delegates either side of her mistress 'in a homely way (*oikeōs*), as becomes a woman' (1118), all the while remaining silent. Then Lysistrata addresses her male onstage audience, briefly spelling out the reasons why she deserves to be listened to ('I am not badly off where intelligence is concerned ... and I am not badly educated', 1125–7) before making a forceful set of points about the current war and how Athens and Sparta should regard one another. The Greeks, she says, share common ancestry – they are 'like family' (*sungeneis*, 1130) – and also have common religious beliefs, worshipping the same gods at sacred sites such as Olympia and

Delphi. Yet they are currently fighting amongst themselves, 'destroying Greek men and cities' (1134), while failing to recognize the threat posed by Persia.[35] As Jeffrey Henderson suggests, Lysistrata's overarching point here can be summarized as follows: 'if you must fight, fight barbarians, not one another', the underlying idea being that 'Athens and Sparta should return to the policy of the good old days'; that is to say, a time when both cities exercised their power in a co-operative way, using it to resist Persia's interference in Greek affairs (see Chapter 1 Section C).[36]

Lysistrata's argument seems clear enough up to this point, but the waters become muddied by what she says next. While the Athenian and Spartan delegates are distracted by the sight of Reconciliation's naked body (as can be judged by their lewd interjections about her appearance: 1136 and 1148), Lysistrata underlines the value of mutual co-operation between the two cities by citing historical instances of Athens and Sparta coming to each other's aid (1137–56). The issue here is that her account of these events is at best selective and at worst revisionist. The first example she gives, the intervention of the Athenian general, Cimon, in the revolt of Sparta's helots (its serf population) in the late 460s BCE did not end well. Not only did the Spartans grow suspicious of his democratically minded Athenian forces and send Cimon back to Athens, but his fellow countrymen also later voted to exile him for his troubles.[37] Lysistrata next recalls the help provided by the Spartan King Cleomenes to overthrow the tyranny of Hippias in Athens in 510 BCE. Something she omits to mention, however, is Cleomenes' return to Athens two years later in a failed attempt to intervene on behalf of opponents of the city's newly established democracy (an event already alluded to by the old men's chorus at lines 274–80). What is impossible to know, of course, is how many members of the original audience would simply have gone with the flow of Lysistrata's argument, seeing these simply as uncomplicated examples of what she calls 'good deeds' initiated by either side in the past (1159), and how many might have recognized and reflected on the partial way in which historical events are presented here.

Lysistrata now ushers in the final stage of the peace negotiations by encouraging the two parties to come to terms. In a piece of staging that has attracted a considerable amount of scholarly attention for the issues it raises about gender and power, the Athenian and Spartan representatives now wrangle over Reconciliation's body which is envisaged as a map of Greece. All the names of territories that the two sides ask for as part of the peace settlement are thinly veiled *double entendres*: as befits the supposed Spartan fondness for anal sex, the representative of Sparta asks for the 'rotunda' of Pylos (1162), a reference to Reconciliation's bottom or anus, whereas the Athenian demands the return of Echinos (or 'Hedgehog', i.e. her pubic hair), the Malian inlet (i.e. her vagina) and the 'Legs' of Megara (a reference to that city's walls, 1169–70).[38] Striking here is the contrast between the active and vocal roles played by the men and the passivity of the mute figure of Reconciliation whose naked body is ogled and systematically divided up between the two sides. In one sense, then, this scene can be viewed as the point at which the men of Greece begin to re-establish control over both the Greek world and the female body – which in this scene are combined in the person of Reconciliation. But it is also striking that the objectification of Reconciliation and the allotment of her body parts are overseen by a woman. It is, after all, Lysistrata who has orchestrated this encounter and who remains in charge of the bargaining process, granting the two sides their sexualized, territorial requests, while exploiting in the most blatant way yet the power of the eroticized, female body to beguile men and distract them from war.[39]

Towards the end of the episode, the action is quickly wrapped up: Lysistrata gains assurances that Athens' and Sparta's allies will agree to the peace terms and the men are then ushered into the Acropolis to exchange oaths in anticipation of a celebration (1182–7).

As they all depart, the unified chorus delivers a further pair of comic odes (1189–1215), repeating the pattern of 1043–71 by making generous offers to all those listening, including any children they might have. Previously these offers were of money and food, this time of sumptuous clothes and large quantities of corn, but in each case the proposition is subsequently undermined: the clothes turn out to be non-existent, for example, and the house in which the grain is kept is guarded by a dog. Kenneth Dover's view of these odes is that they are 'tediously unsophisticated' relying on the repetition of what he calls a 'primitive joke'.[40] However, the chorus' switch to an upbeat and humorous tone is nevertheless significant, paving the way as it does for the cheery atmosphere of the play's resolution. As John Vaio notes, what these songs also mark is a renewed focus on 'household concerns, from which the play took its start'.[41] The themes of clothing, wealth and children that are so important throughout *Lysistrata* reappear here, this time firmly rooted in a domestic context. It is noteworthy, too, how the chorus' empty offer to the audience of free food is juxtaposed with the banquet that the Athenian and Spartan delegates will supposedly enjoy on the Acropolis after agreeing terms. Unlike the spectators in the auditorium, the men of *Lysistrata* – who have negotiated peace – will be able to enjoy its benefits.

(j) Drunken festivities and celebrations (1216–1321)

The final scene of the play is characterized by celebration, upbeat songs and the symbolic reunification of husbands and wives. It begins, however, with two Athenian delegates tumbling out of the *skēnē* doors, following their feasting and drinking on the Acropolis, and drunkenly colliding with the door-keeper (1216). A number of men are evidently gathered outside, and while it is not entirely clear from the text who these silent characters are, their characterization as 'whipping posts' (*mastigiai*) at line 1240 has led scholars to conclude that these must be slaves who arrived with the delegates in the last scene and have been waiting outside for their various masters to emerge.[42] Up to now these slaves have played little part in the action, but here their presence facilitates a self-consciously 'vulgar' (*phortikos*, 1218) slapstick routine, which involves first one delegate then the other threatening to singe their hair with their torches (1217–24, reprised at 1239–40). Following this, the two delegates discuss how successful the drinking party (*sumposion*) was, how charming the Spartans were, and how previous Athenian embassies to Sparta have misunderstood and misrepresented what the Spartans had to say to them. This strikingly forgiving, chirpy assessment of Athens' chief adversary sets much of the tone for the rest of this scene. The Spartan delegates soon come out of the Acropolis (1241), too, and little time is wasted before the theatre is ringing with Spartan song and dance accompanied by the *phusētēria* (or *phuhatēria* in the Laconian dialect, 1242), a typically Spartan form of bagpipes. In his first ode, the Spartan singer recalls Athens' and Sparta's joint successes in the Persian Wars (1249–72) and in his second – which comes at the very end of the transmitted text of the play – he goes on to praise the very glory of Sparta itself (1296–1315).

Arguably, the key point in the midst of all these celebrations is the reunification of the Athenian and Spartan men with their wives – though quite how and when the Spartan wives are supposed to have arrived at the Acropolis is unclear; once more in this comedy, logic gives way to dramatic expediency. It is at lines 1273–8, following the Spartan's first ode, that someone steps forward to enact this symbolic reunion. Addressing the Spartans and Athenians in turn, this speaker instructs each husband and wife to unite and dance together, expressing the hope that Greeks will never again make the mistake of waging war with one another.

Come now, since everything else has been properly taken care of, take these women away, Spartans! And you lot (*to the Athenians*), take *these* women here! Let husband stand by wife and wife by husband, and then let's celebrate these happy events by dancing in honour of the gods – and make sure in the future never to make the same mistake again.

But who is it that speaks these lines? Most modern translators, as well as two key editors of the play – Sommerstein (1990) and Wilson (2007) – opt for Lysistrata, but historically some Aristophanic scholars have instead chosen to give these lines to an Athenian official, a Prytanis, despite the fact that no such figure is mentioned in the text.[43] The 'problem' being addressed by these scholars is not insignificant, namely that there is a certain incongruity involved in a woman taking a commanding role in a scene which sees men reassume their traditional roles as heads of their households and rulers of the city. Not that the proposed solution of such scholars – the introduction of a new male speaker – is without its awkward consequences, since it relies on Lysistrata either being absent at this pivotal moment in the play or, if she is indeed onstage, either standing silently apart from the revellers or being paired up with a husband to whom she is now to be considered subordinate.[44] Sommerstein's suggestion (discussed above), that Lysistrata was presented as something of an Athena figure in these final scenes, provides an ingenious way of ironing out these difficulties: her identification with the virgin goddess would give her an elevated status and make her command of the situation seem all the more natural, while serving to differentiate her from the other married, mortal characters onstage. But whatever the solution, the scholarly debate about the attribution of these lines – and how Lysistrata might have been differentiated from the other women in performance – provides a useful focus for thinking about not only the dynamics of power and gender in this play but also how a powerful female figure like Lysistrata might have been perceived by the original audience (see further Chapter 3 Section A).

The ending of the play has also proven a rich source of discussion. Many scholars have seen the final lines of the text transmitted in our manuscripts – an appeal by the Spartan singer for the chorus to 'sing in praise of the all-conquering goddess, the Mistress of the Bronze House' (1320–1) – as indicating that the original performance of the play would have been rounded off with a hymn to the goddess in question, i.e. Athena (whose bronze – or bronze-clad – temple stood on the Spartan citadel). The failure of copyists to preserve this song in our manuscripts is ascribed to the fact that it was a traditional hymn, i.e. not composed by Aristophanes.[45]

Part of the appeal of the idea of a lost final hymn to Athena no doubt stems from the fact that the text of the play that has come down to us ends with a reference to the goddess as she is worshipped in Sparta ('the Mistress of the Bronze House', 1321) rather than in Athens – an odd note for Aristophanes to strike, perhaps, given the political situation of 411 BCE. Rather than seeing *Lysistrata* as needing an additional element to make it complete, however, Martin Revermann has proposed a more radical solution, namely that the original play might have ended at line 1294 as the chorus dances and exclaims in celebration ('Euoi! Euoi! Euai! Euai!'). Central to Revermann's thesis is that that the final song in the text that has come down to us, in which Sparta's praises are so extensively sung ('Depart lovely Taygetus once more, Spartan Muse, and come . . .', 1296–1321) seems so out of place in a play performed in war-torn Athens that it is more likely to be a later addition – a song composed for a reperformance of the play somewhere other than Athens (the idea he floats is a fourth-century BCE restaging of the play in the Spartan colony of Taras in Southern Italy, 'a true hot spot for theatre' at that time).[46] While this bold suggestion has its appeal, it is nevertheless worth remarking that a song or songs praising Athena would seem far from out of place at the end of *Lysistrata*. After all, this is a goddess who has been repeatedly evoked throughout the play, with the men's and women's respect for her providing an important point of commonality. Yet without the 'Depart lovely Taygetus ...' ode with which our text of the play ends, Athena is absent from *Lysistrata*'s ending, as the pious hymn at 1279–90 that precedes it namechecks a whole series of Olympian deities – Artemis, Apollo, Dionysus, Zeus, Hera and Aphrodite – but fails to mention Athena at all. Thematically, then, it makes good sense for there to be a song at this point in the play that not only honours Athena but also makes a link between her worship at Athens and Sparta, i.e. by reminding the audience of her famous bronze temple in Sparta which, just like Parthenon on Athens' Acropolis, occupied a prime position in the city (this temple is alluded to at line 1299 – 'Athena of the Bronze House' – as well as in the final line of the play). To be sure, it would have been a bold decision for Aristophanes to have his actors perform this ode in front of an Athenian audience in 411 BCE (though its tone is perhaps not wholly out of keeping with Aristophanes' positive treatment of Sparta elsewhere in the play: see Chapter 3 Section B). But importantly, if this song was indeed missing from the original performance, a golden opportunity was missed to use the Athena motif as a fitting and powerful climax to the play. Of course, if Sommerstein is right that Lysistrata appeared in this final scene dressed as Athena, then the goddess herself was in one sense present all along.[47]

People, Places and Politics

(a) Lysistrata: Leader, priestess, wife, warrior, goddess

As one of Aristophanes' most remarkable and memorable creations, Lysistrata has cast quite a spell on scholars of the play. For Edith Hall, she is a 'sophisticated and complex figure' who exudes 'moral and political authority', while for Jeffrey Henderson she is a woman 'endowed with a degree of intelligence, will and eloquence that would have been considered extraordinary in a citizen of either sex'.[1] As we saw in Chapter 2, different strengths of Lysistrata's continue to emerge throughout the play: she is revealed to be a visionary leader, an arch strategist and a persuasive speaker who displays shrewd insight not only into women's concerns but, crucially, into men's behaviour, too. Aristophanes' creation of such a strong, compelling and ultimately sympathetic figure is all the more remarkable given that this was probably the first time that a female character had played such a central and commanding role in a comic play.

As has previously been highlighted, throughout the play Aristophanes subtly positions Lysistrata and her female followers as part of a long tradition of masterful women by drawing on a rich vein of stories from myth and history (see Chapter 1 Section D). Figures referenced in the play – providing points of both comparison and contrast with Lysistrata's women – range from the warrior tribe of Amazons (who besieged the Athenian Acropolis) to the husband-slaying Women of Lemnos (who rose up and took control of their island) and the valiant Queen of Halicarnassus, Artemisia (who excelled on the side of the Persians in the Battle of Salamis).[2] But a further tool Aristophanes uses to endow Lysistrata with authority is to cast her as something of a priestess figure. At first, the association of Lysistrata with organized religion is merely hinted at – through her reference to women's religious festivals in the very first lines of the play (1–3), for example, and various allusions to animal sacrifice in her initial exchange with Lampito (Lysistrata: 'You could throttle a bull!'; Lampito: 'Honestly, you're feeling me over like an animal for sacrifice!' 81–4); towards the end of the prologue she can even be seen officiating over the 'sacrifice' of the wine jar (181–239). Allusions to female religious activities recur throughout the play as does the sacrifice motif – most notably in the reconciliation scene, where Lysistrata once again presides over a mock sacrifice, this time overseeing the imagined division of Reconciliation's body parts between the Athenian and Spartan delegates (1162–72).[3]

A significant moment in the scholarship of this play came in 1955 when David Lewis made a connection between the fictional Lysistrata and a real-life individual, an Athenian woman of aristocratic lineage named Lysimache, who served as the Priestess of Athena Polias ('Athena protectress of the city') in classical Athens.[4] The combined evidence of a literary source from first century CE Rome (Pliny, *Natural History* 34.76) and a fragmentary inscription from fourth-century BCE Athens (IG II² 3453) suggests that Lysimache held this prestigious post for an extraordinary sixty-four years, died at the age of eighty-eight and, following her death, was commemorated with a statue on the Acropolis. Since the sculptor of this statue (Demetrios of Alopeke) was only active until about 360 BCE, it therefore seems likely that Lysimache was Priestess at the time *Lysistrata* was first staged in 411 BCE. Of course, the obvious link between the real-life priestess and the fictional heroine is provided by their names, which are strikingly similar both in form and meaning: Lysimache signifies 'dissolver of battles' and Lysistrata 'dissolver of armies'.[5] Intriguingly, too, the text of *Lysistrata* appears specifically to name this priestess.

During the Magistrate scene Lysistrata declares that, if the sex-strike plot is successful, women will one day be known among the Greeks as Lysimaches, 'the Dissolvers of Battles' (*Lusimachai*, 554).[6] Importantly, too, this reference to Lysimache is a rare example of a 'respectable' woman being named in public by a free man who is not related to her, leading various scholars, such as Jeffrey Henderson, to wonder whether her priesthood and the public role and visibility that came with it 'exempted her from the ordinary protocol'[7] The only other example of a woman in comedy being named in this way is Lysistrata herself towards the end of the play (1086, 1103 and 1147), plausibly indicating that she is also envisaged as enjoying a high public profile, either by virtue of her association with the real-life priestess and/or as a result of the unusual level of power she now enjoys owing to the success of her scheme.[8]

Scholars have highlighted a whole range of elements in the play that fit with Lysistrata being characterized as a Priestess of Athena Polias figure. For instance, the civic and religious status of this role might explain not only Lysistrata's influence over other women, but also the deference that the male characters show her in the closing scenes of the play. The Acropolis setting becomes all the more resonant, too: the Priestess of Athena Polias had a residence there, which allowed her to oversee activities such as the organization of banquets (Lysistrata hosts a feast and celebrations at the end of the play) and the training of her young assistants, the Arrephoroi, who helped to weave the sacred robe, or *peplos*, of Athena for the Panathenaea (this is a role that the chorus of old women claim to have played as girls at line 641). The Priestess' oversight of the manufacture of this garment also links with the weaving imagery that pervades the play, including Lysistrata's famous wool-working metaphor where reforming the citizenry of Athens is envisaged as analogous to turning a tangled skein of wool into a warm, woven cloak (*chlaina*) for the city to wear (574–86: see Chapter 4 Section C). Some commentators on the play have even gone as far as suggesting that, in the closing scene of the play, Lysistrata is characterized not so much as a Priestess of Athena, but as the deity she served, Athena herself (see Chapter 2 Section J).[9]

While most scholars would agree that Lysistrata's characterization is enriched in this play by her association with Lysimache, the relationship between the two figures is nevertheless complex, with Aristophanes apparently taking care to portray Lysistrata as different from the real-life priestess. For instance, one of the play's wives, Calonice – who is evidently not too old to participate in the sex strike herself – greets Lysistrata using the elevated word *teknon*, or 'child' (line 7), a 'form of address [which] requires the addressee to be considerably younger than the speaker'.[10] Yet in 411 BCE, the real-life Lysimache must have been in her late thirties at the very least and possibly much older. In a similar vein, although Lysistrata seems to speak of a husband (*anēr*) at line 513, implying that she is either married or a widow,[11] she does not specifically mention having children, whereas the fragmentary inscription from the Acropolis (see above) suggests that Lysimache was not only a mother, but even 'lived to see four generations of descendants'.[12] There are other elements of Lysistrata's portrayal, too, that perhaps fit awkwardly with the Priestess of Athena Polias role, not least the way Lysistrata suggestively sings Myrrhine's praises to her husband, Cinesias, and later produces the naked Reconciliation to excite and be ogled by the Athenian and Spartan delegates (845–64, 1114). Arguably, then, it is not just because the name 'Lysimache' makes for a poor fit with the iambic rhythms of comedy's spoken sections that Aristophanes chose a different name for his heroine. Rather, Aristophanes has chosen to carve out a distinct personality for his heroine, albeit one that draws liberally on the standing and associations of the Priestess of Athena Polias role.[13]

Lysistrata's distinctiveness is also apparent in the ways she differs from the other Athenian women. It is not only qualities like her strategic and rhetorical prowess that set her apart, but also her relative lack of frivolity and apparent imperviousness to sexual temptation. But this is not to say that she displays no interest in sex. For instance, if lines 107–10 are indeed spoken by Lysistrata, then she even laments the lack of lovers and dildos in the city.[14]

> Really, there's not so much as a glimmer of a lover (*moichos*) left. And ever since the Milesians deserted us, I've not even seen a five-inch dildo – which at least might have brought us *some* artificial relief.

When selling the idea of the sex strike to the other women, Lysistrata also betrays a keen knowledge of what gets men sexually excited – and her use of verbs in the first person plural ('we …') might reasonably be taken to imply that she, too, has been a sexually active wife in the past who now means to join the others in denying her husband sexual gratification (149–54).

> If we sat at home, all made up, wearing nothing but our fine-spun, see-through gowns and we paraded around, plucked down below delta-style, and our husbands got all hard and eager for action, but we kept our distance and didn't go to them, they would make peace quickly enough, I'm sure of it.

This sense of personal involvement in the sex strike is further echoed in the Magistrate scene, when – on behalf of her fellow women – Lysistrata prays for Eros and Aphrodite to 'breathe desire over *our* (*hēmōn*) breasts and thighs' so that Greece's menfolk will suffer from 'bouts of truncheonism' (551–4). Nor does it seem to be just an interest in sex that Lysistrata shares with the wives, but alcohol, too. Following the oath-swearing scene in the prologue, Calonice interjects to prevent Lysistrata from over-indulging in the wine they have sworn over (238–9).

Lysistrata   Here, let me sanctify this cup. (***She starts to drink a long draught.***)

Calonice   Only your fair share, my friend! Let's make sure we're friends with each other right from the start!

One final aspect of Lysistrata's characterization that deserves attention is her attitude towards war and violence. As we will see in Chapter 5, an important strand in the modern reception of this play is its association with pacifist causes. However, as Alan Sommerstein has shown, while Aristophanes' heroine certainly seeks to put an end to the Peloponnesian War, she not only fails to condemn other military conflicts but also actively supports the use of force.[15] The examples that Lysistrata cites in the reconciliation scene of the mutual benefits that Athens and Sparta have brought each other are particularly revealing here, since the intervention of the Athenian general Cimon in the helot revolt in Sparta in 462 BCE and Sparta's role in the end of tyranny at Athens in 510 BCE are both *military* actions (lines 1137–56 and 1149–56). Furthermore, in the Magistrate scene a mere twenty-five lines separate Lysistrata's entrance onstage from the moment when she ferociously unleashes her 'fellow fighters' (*summachoi*, 456) on the Proboulos and his men, crying, 'Go on, manhandle them, hit them, punch them, abuse them, be shameless!' (459–60). To restate, it is the Peloponnesian War in particular that comes under scrutiny in this play and not the notion of military conflict or fighting in general.

Of course, the idea of a powerful female warrior who staunchly defends the Acropolis, who is impervious to sexual temptation – and who is also knowledgeable about wool-working – owes much to the various guises under which Athens' patron deity was worshipped: Athena Promachos ('Athena who fights in front'), Athena Polias ('Athena, guardian of the city'), Athena Parthenos ('Athena the virgin') and Athena Ergane ('Athena the industrious', the goddess of handicrafts, including weaving). But just as there is no easy fit between Lysistrata and the Priestess Lysimache, Lysistrata's association with Athena is felt more strongly in some parts of the play than others. As

Edith Hall has argued, Aristophanes has drawn on stories and traditions associated with a whole range of gender-defying female figures in the creation of his heroine, including but not restricted to Athena and her Priestess. Ultimately, then, Lysistrata is a unique creation designed by Aristophanes to inhabit the particular world of this play and to carry its action. She is a 'clearly drawn, heartwarming and memorable personality' that Aristophanes has skilfully crafted to entertain, challenge, surprise and dazzle his audience.[16]

(b) Sparta and the Spartans

In 411 BCE, the year of *Lysistrata*'s production, the Peloponnesian War was in a critical phase for Athens. Disaster had loomed for the Athenians in 413 BCE after their ill-judged campaign in Sicily (see Chapter 1 Section C). But while the odds were still stacked in favour of Sparta and her allies, some minor Athenian naval victories and the regaining by Athens of some previously lost territory indicated that the city was still a force to be reckoned with. Of course, this real-world war in which so many Athenian men had died and which Athens continued to fight on numerous fronts (as signalled in lines 102–4), is absorbed by Aristophanes into the fictional world of *Lysistrata*, providing the backdrop to – and the motivation for – the women's occupation of the Acropolis and the sex strike.

Given that *Lysistrata* was performed in Athens some twenty years after the initial outbreak of war with Sparta and at a time when the city was pressed so hard, one of its single most remarkable features is the positive way in which it presents Sparta and the Spartans. To take a simple example, in a pause in the celebrations that end the play, an Athenian remarks, 'the Spartans really were so charming!' (*charientes*, 1226) and it is noteworthy that in a play which celebrates peace, it is the Spartans who are the more eager to end the war. It is the Spartans, after all, who send a herald and ambassadors to Athens 'to agree a peace settlement' (*diallagē*, 984, 1102) rather than the other way round – something hardly imaginable in real life in 411 BCE, since the Spartans had the upper hand and the stronger bargaining position. Indeed, in the months that followed the production of *Lysistrata*, Sparta more than once rebuffed Athenian attempts to secure peace, even when the Athenians were prepared to sacrifice their empire to achieve it.[17]

So, does Aristophanes portray the Spartans simply as charming peacemakers? Not quite. The chorus of old men does at least remind the audience of one negative quality connected with Spartans, namely their reputation for deceitfulness, with the assertion that 'Laconian men ... cannot be trusted any more than a ravening wolf' (628–9).[18] Lysistrata provides a further reminder of alleged Spartan dishonesty when, at line 513, she reminds the audience of the Athenian Assembly's decision in 418 BCE to inscribe a footnote to the text of a peace treaty – the treaty that Athens had made with Sparta in 421 BCE, ushering in the Peace of Nicias – to the effect that 'the Spartans have not kept their oaths' (Thucydides 5.56.3).[19] During the reconciliation scene, the Spartan delegate is also quick to admit that Sparta has treated Athens unfairly, telling Lysistrata, 'We are in the wrong' (1147). But none of these points amounts to a straightforward condemnation of Sparta. Indeed, the old men's chorus might be seen as unsympathetic at that point in the play and as voicing an unreasonable prejudice, looking for reasons to prolong the war. Instructively, too, Lysistrata cites the emendation of the peace treaty as an example of a controversial policy decision that the citizen men of Athens had failed to discuss with their wives (indeed, this provocative move ultimately led to a military defeat for Athens at the Battle of Mantinea and put the fragile peace with Sparta at serious risk). The Spartan's admission of wrongdoing, too, which is voiced at a point of extreme sexual desperation on the

Spartan's part, might perhaps be taken as indicating a willingness to compromise, albeit under duress – a conciliatory step to make it easier for the Athenians to make peace.

A particularly fascinating take on Aristophanes' depiction of Sparta comes from examining the presentation of certain historical events in the play. Lysistrata's memory is long and one of the events she mentions during the reconciliation scene is the expulsion of the tyrant Hippias from Athens in 510 BCE (see also Chapter 2 Section I). The account she gives of the end of Hippias' tyranny (1150–6), in which she attributes a decisive role in the liberation of Athens to King Cleomenes of Sparta, is certainly striking. After all, few Athenians would have thought to mention the role of Cleomenes in these events – rather, popular wisdom (as Thucydides 1.20 confirms) was that the tyranny effectively ended when Hippias' brother Hipparchus was slain by two Athenian lovers, Harmodius and Aristogeiton, at Athens' Panathenaea festival in 514 BCE. Indeed, the role of this same-sex couple in founding the democracy was widely celebrated in the classical era. Bronze statues of the pair stood near the centre of the Athenian agora or 'market place' (these are mentioned at line 633 of the play) and the couple's exploits even formed the subject of popular drinking songs, such as that begun by one of the old men at line 632: 'I will carry my sword in a branch of myrtle … like Harmodius and Aristogeiton.'[20]

Another curious description given by Lysistrata is of the mission led by the Athenian general Cimon, sent to help the Spartans following the earthquake of 464 BCE and the subsequent revolt of Sparta's serf population, the helots. Her version of events (1138–44) describes a desperate Sparta saved from near disaster by Athens' timely help. Yet in actual fact (as outlined in Chapter 2 Section I), Cimon's help was ignominiously rejected by Sparta – possibly because the democratic sensibilities of the Athenian troops led them to sympathize with the helots – and the whole debacle ultimately led to his enforced exile from Athens. There is no hint of any of this in Lysistrata's revisionist account.

The way history is presented in the play, then, largely seems to promote the idea that Athens and Sparta had profitably co-operated in the past. This is a view that chimes with Lysistrata's notion of Athenians and Spartans being one family (*sungeneis*, 1130), too, and which is picked up by the Spartan's song about the Persian Wars towards the end of the play (1248–72), where both sides' achievements in the Greek victory over the Persians nearly seventy years before are given equal weight and where prayers are made for lasting unity between the two cities. The one instance of a Spartan hostile to Athens comes at lines 274–80, when the old men's chorus mentions King Cleomenes' occupation of the Acropolis in 508 BCE as part of a military intervention to support opponents of the city's fledgling democracy – but, of course, this is the same Cleomenes who is later credited by Lysistrata with helping to put an end to the tyranny. Intriguingly, then, the negative image of Cleomenes established by the old men early in the play is later revisited by Lysistrata and cast in a more positive light.

There are further ways in which Sparta and Spartans are celebrated in *Lysistrata*. The city was famed for the beauty of its women (Helen of Troy was Spartan), and this positive stereotype is drawn on by Aristophanes in his characterization of Lampito, the one Spartan female introduced in the play. When she arrives at the women's meeting, she is addressed by Lysistrata in the following terms (78–81):

> Lampito, my dearest Laconian friend, welcome! You sweet, sweet woman, what beauty you display! And what a fine colour you are: your body is simply bursting with health. You could throttle a bull!

To which Calonice adds (83):

> What a great pair of tits you've got!

As Lampito readily informs us, her healthy body has been acquired through exercise ('I work out a lot and do heel-to buttock jumps', 82) – a reminder, if the Athenian audience needed one, that Spartan girls underwent a similar physical training regime to that of Spartan boys.[21] Lampito's costume may well have been more revealing than those of her Athenian counterparts, too (in Euripides' *Andromache*, Peleus claims that Spartan women have loose morals and leave the house in the company of young men 'in loose-fitting *peploi* with their thighs exposed': line 598).[22] This focus on the looks and prowess of Spartan women is later echoed in the song which ends the text of the play, too, where the city's 'maidens' are said to dance 'beside the River Eurotas like fillies, moving nimbly, raising clouds of dust with their feet ... with Leda's daughter (i.e. Helen) out in front, the sacred and beautiful leader of the chorus' (1307–15). By dwelling on the beauty and athleticism of its women, then, Aristophanes has arguably chosen to emphasize features of Spartan civilization that would have been attractive and exotic to his spectators. Spartans were also celebrated for their achievements in the area of song and dance, and so it is noteworthy that these pursuits are prominently showcased in the celebrations that end the play. Here we find a Spartan singer who dances the Spartan 'two-step' (*dipodia*) to a tune played on the Spartan bagpipes (1242–3) and whose final song cheerfully praises his city (1296–1315). As this Spartan embarks on his first song-and-dance routine, one of the Athenian onlookers even anticipates a possible response by the members of Aristophanes' audience when he admiringly comments, 'How I enjoy watching you people dance!' (1246).

A further notable feature of Aristophanes' portrayal of Sparta is the way in which he embeds local Spartan colour in the play. For instance, in the prologue of the play, Aristophanes has Lampito allude to Laconia's imposing Mount Taygetus (the Peloponnese's highest peak, line 117), the city's most notorious mythical inhabitants, Helen and

Menelaus (155–6), and even the detachable strap characteristic of Spartan shields (the *porpax*, 106). The closing song likewise evokes Mount Taygetus and Helen as well as various local sights, including the Eurotas river and Athena's bronze temple on Sparta's Acropolis (1301 and 1308; 1299 and 1321). The Spartans' dress and physical appearance would presumably have provided the original audience with visual reminders of their distinctive identity, too, though attention is rarely called to these in the text. Exceptions include the women's discussion of Lampito's physique and a reference to lengthy beards sported by the Spartan delegates (1072), which were presumably accompanied by the long hair for which Spartan men were renowned.[23] Spartan disdain for Athenian democracy is also alluded to momentarily, neatly encapsulated in Lampito's reference to the common Athenian 'rabble' (*rhuacheton*, 170) whom she fears Lysistrata will be unable to make see sense.[24]

A final point to consider about Aristophanes' presentation of Spartans is the Greek they speak in the play. The dialect of Sparta – Laconian – differed from the Attic Greek spoken in Athens just as many dialects of English differ from one another, with divergences in pronunciation, vocabulary, syntax, and so on; not that the Spartan dialect has been straightforward for scholars to reconstruct owing to the fact that so few sources written in Laconian survive.[25] What scholarly analyses of the Greek spoken by the Spartans in *Lysistrata* have concluded, however, is that Aristophanes' representation of Laconian Greek, while not altogether faultless, is nevertheless highly accomplished. Indeed, in his painstaking study of Aristophanes' attempts at rendering a range of different Greek dialects in his plays, Stephen Colvin's considered view is that 'Laconian is the dialect depicted most carefully by the playwright'.[26] Some of the more pronounced features of Laconian dialect include: the frequent occurrence of *ā* where Attic Greek has *ē* (thus *kārux*, 'herald', rather than *kērux* at line 983); *dd* where Attic uses *z* (*gumnaddomai*, 'I exercise, work out', rather than *gumnazomai* at 82), and sigma where Attic Greek has theta (thus *parsene sia*, 'virgin goddess', rather than *parthene thea*, at 1263, the sigma (*s*) employed in an attempt to represent the idiosyncratic Laconian use of the sound 'th', as in in 'thin', in their dialect, at a time when speakers of Attic and other Greek dialects generally pronounced the Greek letter theta as 't^h' in 'pothole'). Not that the Spartans' Greek in *Lysistrata* is stereotype free: there are liberal scatterings of *oiō*, 'I think, I reckon', and the oath *nai tō siō*, 'by the two gods' (a reference to Castor and Pollux, the brothers of Helen), which Aristophanes clearly regarded as distinctive Laconianisms.[27] These accompany a flurry of other distinctly non-Attic words and grammatical forms, including *lō*, 'I wish', *kala*, 'ships' and *hames*, 'we'. The relative accuracy of the Laconian written by Aristophanes has led at least one scholar to wonder how he became so familiar with the dialect: did he travel to Sparta, perhaps, at a time when relations between his city and theirs had been less fraught?[28] Whatever the answer, an important point to make is that Aristophanes had a golden opportunity to mock the way in which Spartans spoke – by making them appear incomprehensible, stupid or unsophisticated – but clearly chose not to take it.[29]

As we have seen, this failure to mock the speech of the Spartans forms part of a broader picture in which Aristophanes generally chooses to represent Sparta and Spartans in a positive light. Nor is this true only of *Lysistrata*. As David Harvey concludes in 'Lacomica', his study of Aristophanes' portrayal of Sparta across all his surviving plays, 'Aristophanes treats the Spartans rather gently, tones down or even supresses certain unpleasantness, and even expresses admiration for them'.[30] But this approach should not necessarily be taken to indicate pro-Spartan leanings on the part of Aristophanes (see Section C below). Indeed, from the limited evidence that can be culled from the fragments of other fifth-century BCE comedies, it seems that Aristophanes' rival playwrights also refrained from stinging criticism of Sparta, which might suggest that other factors are at play. For Ralph Rosen, for example, Aristophanes' objectives as a satirist have a strong bearing on this issue since, he proposes, it is the abuse of wealth and power by those *in Athens* – rather than citizens of other city-states – that Old Comic playwrights ultimately seek to expose and attack.[31] In the context of *Lysistrata*, however, surely an important point to make is that the positive press received by Sparta and the Spartans – regardless of whether or not any given audience member thought it appropriate or justified – serves a dramatic purpose, too, namely to bolster the appeal of the ideology promoted in the reconciliation scene. Here, of course, Lysistrata champions the benefits of Panhellenic co-operation – a notion which is underpinned by the numerous references in the play to the glory days of the Persian Wars, when Athens, Sparta and other Greek states stood united against a common enemy. Put simply, the idea of making peace with Sparta, celebrating a mutually supportive past and looking forward to a common future has far more appeal if the Spartans can be painted as historic allies and attractive people with a vibrant culture to share.

(c) Seriously funny? *Lysistrata* and politics

There is no escaping the fact that *Lysistrata* is a deeply political play. It takes as its starting point the contemporary city (*polis*) of Athens and touches on some of its citizens' most pressing concerns. In the play, it is foreign policy that Lysistrata's scheme is designed to impact most: her stated objectives are to put an end to the Peloponnesian War, promote co-operation between Athens and Sparta, and encourage others to recognize and resist the threat posed by Persia to the Greek-speaking world (see Chapter 2 Section I). But Lysistrata has plenty to say about how affairs are conducted within Athens, too. She has complaints about the quality of decision-making in the city, the machinations of self-serving individuals, and the lack of preparedness of Athens' citizen men to engage with a key demographic excluded from public policy-making, namely its women (see Chapter 2 Section D).

A reasonable question to ask of these views of Lysistrata is what they represent. Whilst there are, as we shall see, competing and compelling ways to interpret Lysistrata's complaints and the objectives of her scheme, most scholars would no doubt distance themselves from the idea that Aristophanes necessarily shared all her grievances and ambitions himself. After all, why should we assume that Aristophanes felt the need to have a given character in a play faithfully represent his own opinions? And in any case, which of Lysistrata's views could we reasonably think that Aristophanes might have shared? Perhaps he did see Persia as a threat and/or Sparta as a potential ally, but did he also believe that women ought to be consulted about decisions made in the city's Assembly – or lament the scarcity of dildos in the city, as Lysistrata does at lines 109–10? But this is not to say that many of the points made by Lysistrata and others in the play – about the effects of war and the plight of women, for example – are presented in anything other than a heartfelt way. Indeed, at times Aristophanes positively encourages the notion that his characters are airing considered, personal viewpoints by having them specifically claim to be offering 'good advice' to the city and its leaders. This happens on three occasions, in fact, and interestingly it is always female characters who stake a claim to be offering 'useful words' or 'good advice' when outlining their views on how Athens should be run. Lysistrata claims that the women will propose 'useful things' (*chrēsta*, line 527), for example, a sentiment the chorus of old women later echo, declaring they will offer 'useful words' (*logōn ... chrēsimōn*, 638–9) and say 'something useful' to the city (*ti chrēston*, 648). Crucially, then, Lysistrata's women offer no shortage of thought-provoking points for the male-dominated theatre audience to consider – and do so, we might note, in a play where men are repeatedly cast as foolish for failing to heed women's advice in the past (see Chapter 2 Section D).

Needless to say, the peace that Lysistrata ultimately secures for Athens hardly represents a real-world solution to Athens' troubles in 411 BCE; rather, it belongs firmly to the world of fantasy. After all, this settlement with Sparta is achieved in both an extraordinarily swift timeframe and in a conveniently face-saving manner, requiring the city's men neither to make the first move nor to offer any substantial concessions to their former enemy (indeed the territorial settlement made at lines 1162–72 is extremely advantageous to the Athenians compared with what they might realistically have hoped for in real life).[32] Importantly, too, the return to the Good Old Days of Panhellenic co-operation which comes towards the end of the play – and which is celebrated in a finale featuring plentiful food and wine as well as the promise of sex – sits within a broader tradition of exuberant 'happy endings' found in other Old Comic plays. Aristophanes' *Peace*, for example, enacts and celebrates an end to the Peloponnesian War (this was a play produced in 421 BCE at a time when, in the real world, the Peace of Nicias was close to being agreed: see Chapter 1 Section B). In *Archarnians* (425 BCE), too, Dicaeopolis succeeds in obtaining and then celebrates his own personal peace treaty with Sparta (in justification of which, we might note, he appeals to the audience not to lay all the fault for the conflict at the door of Sparta: *Acharnians* 509–56). In this light, the reconciliation with Sparta that is sought and secured in *Lysistrata* might be viewed not so much as a meaningful policy for the city to pursue in 411 BCE as a well-worn comic trope – a time-honoured plot device which provides Aristophanes with a conveniently upbeat and celebratory conclusion to his play.

The pro-peace and pro-Spartan stances we find in *Lysistrata* are not the only 'political' positions we find recurring in Aristophanes' work. Lysistrata's criticism of the Assembly and its decision-making forms part of a broader pattern, too. Famously, in comedies written in less politically charged times than *Lysistrata*, this hostility towards the prevailing political system in Athens regularly extends to personal attacks on politicians – or at least democrat politicians, i.e. those who champion and rely on the support of Athens' lower classes; interestingly, politicians whose allegiances lay with the city's more socially and politically conservative aristocracy are characteristically spared.[33] Naturally, the question then arises of how to account for this anti-democrat/pro-aristocrat bias. Since we have no evidence beyond his surviving plays to indicate what Aristophanes actually thought about contemporary issues in Athenian society, we cannot rule out the possibility that his personal views aligned more with those of aristocrats than with those of democrats (like many of his fellow poets, he was a member of Athens' social elite, after all). However, other explanations for Old Comedy's political leanings are potentially more compelling. Studies of the audiences of Old Comedy, for example, tend to conclude that the demographics of spectators in the theatre would have been skewed in favour of wealthy, urban Athenians.[34] So might these 'elite' biases that we find in Old Comedy be best accounted for as an attempt by playwrights to appeal to their audiences' tastes and prejudices? Alternatively, if Old Comic poets are to be regarded as offering a distinctive kind of humorous scrutiny of the city at the comic festivals each year – providing not just laughter in their plays, but biting satire, too – then it arguably makes sense that the personalities of those in power, their policies (including, in the late fifth century BCE, the continuation of the war with Sparta), and the workings of the Athens' civic institutions (including the Assembly and its decision-making) should be subject to criticism and ridicule. Or, in other words, the political biases to be found in Old Comedy might usefully be seen as anti-establishment rather than anti-democrat per se, with the abuse and mockery of the city's leaders,

institutions and policies all part and parcel of the particular approach
to satire that Old Comic poets took. It should also be said that these
various approaches to understanding the political leanings of
Aristophanes' plays – the biographical, the audience-orientated and
the genre-related – are not mutually exclusive, and over the years
different scholars have foregrounded or downplayed the importance
of each in their explorations of this contentious topic.[35]

So far we have mainly been considering large-scale political biases
in Aristophanic comedy: its pro-elite and anti-establishment stance,
for example, and its tendency to use peace and resolution to underpin
a celebratory ending. But to return to the subject of 'good advice', there
are also moments in the play when Lysistrata offers up some fairly
specific thoughts about the policy directions that the *polis* of Athens
should adopt in the future. The most developed set of such
recommendations comes during Lysistrata's encounter with the
Proboulos, where her proposed solutions to the city's problems are
presented in the form of a lengthy simile-cum-metaphor drawing on
the play's theme of wool-working (see Chapter 2 Section D). At first,
Lysistrata likens solving the city's problems to untangling a skein of
wool, her comparison leading her to suggest sending embassies 'first
this way, then that' (570), presumably to sue for peace. Extending the
wool analogy, she goes on to lay out a whole series of proposals for
internal political reform in the city (574–86):

First of all, just like a raw fleece, you have to wash the sheep-dung
out of the city in a bath, then putting it on a bed, bash out the
villains with a rod and pick off the burrs – and as for those who
combine and who mat themselves together for political gain, you
should card them out and pluck off their heads. Then card general
goodwill into a basket, mixing everyone together: the immigrants
(*metoikoi*), any foreigner who is friendly to you, and anyone who is
in debt to the public treasury – mix them in, too. And, by Zeus,
don't forget the cities that are colonies of this land: you should

recognize that these are lying around all by themselves like flocks of wool. So, from each of these you should take the citizen-flock, bring them together here and join them all together to make one big ball of wool from which you can then weave a nice warm cloak for the people to wear.

In this speech, Lysistrata suggests that 'villains' and 'those who combine and who mat themselves together for political gain' should be removed from the citizen body: here the target seems to be public figures who belong to (anti-democratic) political factions and/or who collude to gain money and power (compare the complaints made against Peisander and other unnamed men at lines 490–2).[36] Next she mentions groups who, she says, should be included in the citizenry but are currently excluded. Four groups are mentioned: (i) 'metics' or resident immigrants (*metoikoi*); (ii) any foreigner (*xenos*) who is well-disposed (*philos*) to the city; (iii) debtors (who were disenfranchised at Athens, hence the need for the reinstatement of their citizen rights); and (iv) Athens' colonies. The precise make-up of some of these groups is challenging to pin down. What 'foreigners' does she mean exactly? And what does she mean by 'colonies' (*poleis . . . apoikoi*, 582)? Plausibly, this refers not just to recently founded 'colonies' in the strict sense of the term, but to (loyal) subject states in the Aegean and Asia Minor whose Ionic Greek ethnic and linguistic heritage was traditionally thought to stem from their foundation by Athens.[37] These complications aside, however, the gist of what Lysistrata is proposing is clear enough: namely, sweeping reforms to allow multiple groups of men allied to the Athenian state, but currently excluded from citizenship, to be incorporated into its citizen body.

Lysistrata's suggestions in her speech are certainly striking and, perhaps, in the recent years of crisis following the failure of the Sicilian Expedition, Athenians had grown used to radical proposals for wide-reaching reform (indeed, as mentioned in Chapter 1 Section B, revolutionary change was soon to be imposed on Athens in the form of an oligarchic coup which took place just a few months after *Lysistrata* was staged). But the sending of embassies aside, could any of them have been taken seriously in contemporary Athens? Once again, we are faced with the problem of how to understand and interpret political 'advice' which is ostensibly presented in earnest, but which does not quite stand up to scrutiny in the real world – not least because Lysistrata seems to be suggesting quick-fix, sweeping solutions to what in 411 BCE were no doubt a highly complex and largely intractable set of problems. Interestingly, too, there seems to be little connection between Lysistrata's proposals here and her broader plans in the play, where it is women's control of two crucial spaces – the Athenian Acropolis and their own bodies – which is set to deliver a happy ending for Athens, not an expansion of its male citizen ranks.[38] But the very fact that Aristophanes is using an Old Comic play to address political issues – rather than, say, a speech in the city's Assembly – means that he is perfectly at liberty to mix humour, fantasy and exuberance into Lysistrata's proposals and can legitimately float ideas that are not just thought-provoking, but also eye-catching, controversial and even eccentric. Put another way, a comic poet might reasonably be expected to entertain the members of his audience, but he is under no obligation to provide them with practical and workable solutions to real-world problems.[39]

None of this has prevented scholars from offering political readings of *Lysistrata*, of course. In line with the arguments put forward by Lysistrata both in the reconciliation scene and elsewhere, the play is commonly viewed as an appeal for peace and Pan-Hellenic co-operation – as well a more measured form of democracy. Sommerstein, for example, sums up what he calls 'Aristophanes' political creed' – covering both foreign and domestic policy – in the following way:[40]

Abroad, peace, to be followed by a league of all the Greek states under the leadership of Athens and Sparta, which should be prepared for a possible renewal of the struggle against Persia; at home, preferably a democracy tempered by deference, which should listen to the advice of the well-born, rich and educated.

This notion of the play as supporting a conservative form of democracy, with 'well-born' leaders steering public affairs, is explored by other scholars, too. Kate Gilhuly, for example, makes much of the fact that Lysistrata's characterization draws on the figure of Lysimache, the Priestess of Athena Polias (see Chapter 3 Section A), a position which was the preserve of women from one of Athens' oldest, noble families, the Eteoboutadai.[41] In a similar vein, as she points out, the chorus of old women reveal connections to Athens' upper classes when they talk about the role they played in their youth in a series of religious roles in honour of various goddesses – Arrephoros, Grinder, Bear and basket-bearer in the city's Panathenaea procession – since all these positions were reserved for the daughters of Athens' elite (641–7).[42] Lysistrata and the chorus of old women thus contrast with many of the other women in the play, who are drawn from different parts of the social spectrum, such as the lower-class traders – the hard-headed market vendors and inn-keepers – that Lysistrata calls on in lines 457–8 to come to her aid. What *Lysistrata* therefore models, Gilhuly suggests, is a city controlled and effectively run by the social elite – an elite with whom the lower classes willingly and effectively co-operate, accepting their subordinate role in the social hierarchy.[43]

Peter Thonemann also provides a reading of the play which places the identification of Lysistrata with the Priestess of Athena Polias at its heart. In his article 'Lysimache and *Lysistrata*', he explores the possibility that Lysimache might in real life have voiced concerns about recent policies pursued by the democracy in Athens, especially the Assembly's bold decision in 412 BCE to spend the city's emergency reserves on re-equipping its fleet (see Chapter 1

Section B). This set of events, Thonemann proposes, might have inspired Aristophanes to create a play where an outspoken priestess figure not only states her objections to current civic policies but also goes further still, actively intervening in the city's affairs to prevent Athens' leaders from spending funds on the war. For Thonemann, then, *Lysistrata* is a topical and provocative play which 'respond[s] in the most direct possible fashion' to what he sees as 'the hottest political issue of its day'.[44] Interestingly, however, he does not see *Lysistrata* as advocating reconciliation between Athens and Sparta. 'If . . . *Lysistrata* is a serious plea for anything,' he suggests, 'it is for better management (particularly financial management) of the war, not peace.'[45]

A different approach again to understanding the politics of *Lysistrata* is provided by Douglas Olson in his article '*Lysistrata*'s Conspiracy and the Politics of 412 BC'. Olson emphasizes the importance of certain complaints voiced by Lysistrata, namely that men have steadfastly refused to discuss public policy with their wives and listen to their views (see Chapter 2 Section D). As he points out, the women have a litany of grievances about the workings of the democracy, whereas the chorus of old men, he argues, are shown to be clinging on to an unhelpful (if ostensibly 'democratic') view of the past which blinds them to their own best interests, not least when it comes to relations with Sparta. 'Once gender is removed from the equation as a comic red herring,' Olson suggests, the women can be seen as 'an indeterminately large group of loyal citizens who nonetheless insist that the current way of governing the city is unacceptable' – a group which has previously been sidelined and ignored.[46] In this light, *Lysistrata*'s women can be seen as representing the disempowered in Athens, whose voices are finally heard and who succeed in bringing about significant political change in the city. For Olson, then, the play represents what would have been an appealing fantasy for many average citizens in the theatre audience;

that is to say, a world where those in power are forced to listen to what the silent majority have to say. However, for Olson this is not the same as seeing the play as a rallying call: indeed, he concludes by saying that *Lysistrata* cannot be 'easily read as a genuine proposal for political action'.[47]

Laughter, Language and Logic

(a) Making Athens laugh: *Lysistrata*'s humour

Whatever the original audience's expectations might have been when they settled down to watch *Lysistrata*, one thing is for certain: they would have anticipated that Aristophanes' play would make them laugh. A more thoughtful spectator might have conceivably wondered how he would manage this. How would an Old Comic playwright like Aristophanes, whose humour so often relied on the mockery of his fellow Athenians, negotiate the thorny political climate of 411 BCE? The answer, it would transpire, was to produce a play which deftly avoids singling out any one named individual for causing Athens' ills (rather it is male citizens in general who are to blame for the continuing war) and which contains only a handful of relatively mild jibes aimed at real-life contemporaries of Aristophanes.[1] Rather than rely on personal abuse, then, Aristophanes has the bulk of the humour in *Lysistrata* grow out of the sex strike and the gendered behaviour of the two sexes whose conflict lies at the play's heart.

At this stage, it is worth pausing briefly to consider the relationship between humour and laughter. On the one hand, 'humour' serves as a convenient umbrella term for describing those elements in the text or action of the play which have the potential to be found funny, witty or amusing by a spectator. As this definition suggests, 'humour' is a broad category, capable of describing moments when an ancient audience might have roared with laughter – such as the arrival of Cinesias sporting an enormous, erect phallus, perhaps? – as well as gentle quips and subtle puns, such as the old men's assertion in the parodos that the

smoke that is bothering them must come from a Lemnian fire (*Lēmnion
. . . pur*, 299) since it is causing 'secretions' in their eyes (*lēmas*, 301).
'Laughter', on the other hand, is a physiological phenomenon which
can arise from a range of different stimuli, including but not restricted
to humour (other catalysts include tickling, relief and social
awkwardness). Importantly, then, even when there is good reason to
believe that a given line, word or sequence in a theatrical text is
'humorous', with the potential to be found amusing, factors such as the
actor's delivery of a line and the audience's mood at a given moment in
the performance will inevitably have a significant impact on how
spectators respond. Or as Stephen Halliwell so concisely puts it,
laughter depends on 'the active collaboration of audiences in
responding to and fulfilling the strategies of humour enacted on stage'.[2]

Obviously, 'humour' and 'laughter' are English terms, and it is worth
noting that the terminology used by ancient Greek writers when
discussing comedy often serves to blur categories that modern
students of Aristophanes might choose to keep distinct. Thus, in
Greek, *geloios*, 'laughter-inducing', 'laughable', 'funny' – related to *gelōs*,
'laughter' – is regularly used to describe what modern scholars might
call 'humorous' material; and what is more, *to geloion*, literally 'that
which induces laughter', is even used casually as a synonym for
comedy itself (*kōmōidia*).[3] (In English, too, the vocabulary of humour
is notoriously slippery: take the word 'comic', for example, which –
amongst other things – can be used *both* to label a line or sequence as
'humorous' or 'funny' *and* to mean 'connected with comedy', as in
'comic poet' or 'comic drama'.) In one sense it seems fair enough to
think of comedy as characteristically 'laughter-inducing', of course –
this is what distinguishes it from other genres such as tragedy, after
all.[4] Yet it is more accurate to say of a comedy like *Lysistrata* that, while
some of its episodes and sequences are simply brimming with
(potentially laughter-inducing) humour, other parts of the play are
not. Lysistrata's comments to the Proboulos about the impact of war

on women, for example, or her speech to the Athenian and Spartan ambassadors about the benefits of Panhellenic co-operation contain no discernible humour (lines 588–97 and 1111–35 respectively). In short, any laughter induced in a theatre audience watching *Lysistrata* would inevitably come in waves, concentrated in some parts of the play and absent from others. As well as being laugh-out-loud funny, Old Comedy can be sombre and sober, too.

Theories of humour date back at least as far as Aristotle and tend to take one of three main approaches to the phenomenon. These are social theories, typically focusing on humour's ability to deride and attack others; psychological theories, which view humour as offering release and liberation, e.g. from the normal constraints of logic and social propriety; and cognitive theories.[5] This last group of theories regard humour as a special kind of incongruity, with listeners typically presented with one way of understanding a situation, word or phrase and then offered an alternative way to decode what they have heard or seen, forcing them to re-evaluate their initial expectations. While such models are often more straightforward to apply to individual jokes than an extended and complex performance text like *Lysistrata*,[6] the following extract from the prologue of the play nevertheless serves to demonstrate how incongruity can underpin humour. Here, Lysistrata has just bemoaned the fact that the other women have not yet arrived at the meeting, prompting Calonice to question her reasons for summoning them (lines 21–4).

Calonice What on earth is it, Lysistrata dear, that are you are calling us women together for? What is this thing? How large is it?

Lysistrata It's big.

Calonice You're not saying it's . . . meaty as well?

Lysistrata Yes, by Zeus: meaty, too.

Calonice Then how come we're not all here?

The humour in these lines is based on a set of *double entendres*. On the one hand, there is an innocent way of understanding 'how large ...?' (*pēlikon*), 'big' (*mega*) and 'meaty' (*pachu*, literally 'thick') as simply referring to a 'matter' or 'thing'; but on the other, there is a sexual reading alongside this, where size, bigness and thickness can be taken as referring to a penis. Calonice's final line builds on the joke and amplifies the *double entendre* further for anyone in the audience who is slow on the uptake: 'big' and 'thick' penises, she points out, are something that women (who are stereotypically sex-mad) ought to be enthusiastic to turn out to discuss.

Double entendres like this one provide a rich seam of humour in *Lysistrata*. They appear in contexts ranging from racy one-liners, such as Myrrhine's reference in the prologue to the Boeotian woman's 'fine low-lying region' (line 88), to short speeches, such as the Spartan's description of the desperate situation in his city ('The whole of Sparta has *risen up* ... we need a *thrust* up country', 995–6) and longer sequences still.[7] These include the chorus' taunting of the Spartan and Athenian delegates as they try to hide their erections ('This situation has *hardened* terribly', 1078) and the Magistrate's descriptions of how husbands unwittingly invite their wives to be seduced by tradesmen, by saying things like (416–19):[8]

> Shoemaker, it's my wife's foot – the strap is hurting her little tushtie, which is so tender; so could you come over in the middle of the day and loosen it up to make the (w)hole thing wider?

Double entendres rely on the co-presence of an obscene and non-obscene meaning in the same word or phrase: 'low-lying region' (*pedion*, 88), 'hardened' (*neneurōtai*, 1078), and so on. But Aristophanes also creates humour through the surprise introduction of blatant sexual references or unambiguously obscene language into formal situations and elevated sequences, thereby creating an incongruous juxtaposition of high- and low-register speech. In real life, the swearing of an oath would be a solemn occasion, for example, but in *Lysistrata* the pledges that the women are asked to make in the prologue are shot through with bawdy elements: 'with a hard-on', 'raise my Persian slippers towards the ceiling', and so on (214–15, 229–30). Likewise the international peace negotiations overseen by Lysistrata feature incongruously obscene interjections from the Athenian and Spartan Delegates as they ogle the body of Reconciliation: 'My boner is killing me'; 'How unspeakably beautiful that arse is' (1136, 1148). High-register sequences, too, can be punctured by low-register language, such as the risqué words that appear in the text of the oracle that Lysistrata reads out to the other women – 'penises' (*phalētōn*, 771); '(more of a) butt-spreading slut' (*katapugōnesteron*, 776) – or the obscenity which brings the tragic-style exchange between Lysistrata and the chorus of old women to abrupt end: 'To summarize our tale: we need a *fuck!*', *binētiōmen*, 715). There is also humorous shock value in the various threats and obscenities uttered by the old women, as exemplified by the warning delivered by a companion of Lysistrata's to the Proboulos – 'if you lay so much as a hand on her, you'll get such a thrashing you'll *shit* yourself!' (*epichesei*, 439–40; on the significance of this obscenity, see Section B below).

This last example introduces another common way in which Aristophanes creates humour in *Lysistrata*, namely by having his female characters depart from the behaviour that might be expected of 'respectable' citizen women in real life.[9] Instead, he often has them conform to comic stereotypes, with the older women regularly portrayed as aggressive and vulgar and the younger women as fixated on sex, with further humorous capital made out of women's supposed fondness for alcohol. Some sequences make generous use of these stereotypes, such as the various confrontations between the two semi-choruses in which the old women defy the old men ('Come on, here you are: someone strike [my cheek]! … And then no other bitch will ever grab your *bollocks* again!', 362–3); the reaction of the younger women to Lysistrata's suggestion of a sex strike ('I would rather walk through fire, too', 136); and the keenness of the women to drink from the cup in the oath-swearing scene ('Let me be the first to swear, ladies!', 207). But Aristophanes also uses these stereotypes as the basis of one-liners, such as Lysistrata's double-edged command to the women after they have defeated the Proboulos and his archers: 'No stripping the bodies!' (461);[10] or the Proboulos' preparedness to agree with Lysistrata that women do indeed display plenty of courage – at least, that is, if they have been fuelled by a 'nearby wineshop' (466).

So far, the discussion has centred on the verbal elements of Aristophanes' play, but the visual aspect is equally important from the point of view of humour – not that the verbal and the visual can be easily separated in a genre designed for physical performance. Indeed, a number of the examples of verbal humour we have already considered in this discussion have clear potential to be enhanced by movement and gesture, such as the horrified reaction of the women to Lysistrata's suggestion that they should abstain from sex (124) or the chorus' mockery of the Athenian delegates, who first desperately try to hide, but soon reveal, their swollen erections ('if you're wise you'll pick up your cloaks in case one of the hermclipper crew sees you', 1093–4: a reference to the Mutilation of the Herms, see Chapter 1 Section B). A notable feature of Aristophanes' script – written as it was to be performed in a large open-air theatre – is that the characters regularly describe actions that a spectator sitting far away from the actors might not easily be able to see. Thus, after proposing her plan for a sex strike, Lysistrata asks the reluctant women 'Why are your turning your backs on me?' (125), and the chorus signals the arrival of the beleaguered Athenian ambassadors by saying: 'Look! I see these men ... standing like wrestlers, holding their cloaks away from their stomachs' (1082–4).

An obvious point to be made about the humorous mockery of the Athenian ambassadors is that it forms part of a larger set of visual 'hard-on' gags in the latter half of play: for Aristophanes, the men's aching erections are the humorous gift that keeps on giving. Cinesias is the first character to emerge sporting a large erect phallus ('Oh, wretched me! What spasms and stiffness seize me .. ', 845), followed by the Spartan Herald ('A human being or a phallic god?', 982).[11] Subsequently, a group of similarly afflicted Spartan delegates arrive ('Why do we need to say many words to you? You can see full well the state we've arrived in', 1076-7) who, in a comic flourish, let their cloaks drop to reveal their protruding phalluses just as the Athenian delegates arrive. Nor is this the only humorous meme to be found in *Lysistrata*. The tussles between the male and female semi-choruses provide a continuous source of visual (as well as verbal) humour throughout the play; as does the theme of combative and well-organized women outwitting inept and ineffectual men: the Proboulos' archers are comprehensively overcome by Lysistrata's companions (456-61), for example, and the Proboulos himself is later humiliated by being dressed as a corpse (599-610). Recurring jokes and joke-types can be detected on a smaller scale, too. For instance, the seduction scene sees Myrrhine repeatedly bringing new objects on stage, ostensibly to aid, but with the ultimate effect of hindering, her love-making with Cinesias (916-51). And in the parodos, the frailty and ineptitude displayed by the old men, as they struggle onstage with their heavy logs (291) and are overpowered by the smoke coming from the fire in their pot (295-305), also hold considerable, ongoing potential for physical humour. Memorably, the men are eventually doused in water by the women (381) – a piece of visual humour that Aristophanes clearly judged to be a humorous highpoint, since the audience is twice reminded of it subsequently (400-2 and 469-70). For Aristophanes, a good joke could clearly bear repeating.

Given the prevalence of visual gags in *Lysistrata*, it is interesting to note that elsewhere in Aristophanes' plays physical humour is often presented as a low form of comedy, typically employed by 'vulgar' (*phortikos*) comic poets simply to elicit laughter – with Aristophanes, in contrast, presenting himself as someone who uses 'skilful' (*dexios*) and 'clever' (*sophos*) words (comments like these tend to emerge in direct addresses to the audience, which are almost entirely absent from *Lysistrata*). This might seem like an odd stance to take for a comic poet who relies so heavily on visual humour, and there is a genuine question here as to what extent these views are heartfelt, playful or posturing on Aristophanes' part and/or simply part of a broader tendency of old comic poets to claim intellectual superiority over their rivals. There is a glimpse of this rhetoric towards the end *Lysistrata*, too, where an Athenian, emerging from the Acropolis after the drunken banquet hosted by the women, threatens to burn some slaves with his torch (1216–20).[12]

> Why are you sitting there, you lot? You don't want me to burn you with my torch, do you? Vulgar routine, that. I won't do it. (**protests from the audience**) Well, if I really have to, I'll make that sacrifice just to indulge you!

This extract shows how Aristophanes skilfully manages here to have his cake and eat it: this coarse slapstick routine gets written off by the character (in what is presented as a metatheatrical exchange with the audience) as a 'vulgar routine' (*phortikon … chōrion*, 1218) – and yet the slaves still get pursued and threatened by him. Crucially, then, this short sequence serves as a useful example in miniature of how Aristophanes seeks to appeal to a broad range of sensibilities in his audience. By using humorous techniques ranging from 'vulgar' slapstick (threatening and chasing the slave) to 'clever' and 'skilful' verbal play ('I won't do it. … Well, if I really have to …!'), his play seems to be geared to making the whole of Athens laugh.

(b) The language of *Lysistrata*: Idiom, obscenity and gender

Anyone coming to *Lysistrata* expecting what scholars have described as the 'dizzyingly inventive' and 'exuberant' expression typical of many other Aristophanic comedies is in danger of being disappointed.[13] Linguistic inventiveness and exuberance are not entirely absent, but while *Lysistrata* can still boast the occasional comic list (e.g. the roll call of Lysistrata's qualities at 1108–9, 'forceful, gentle, noble, ordinary, …'), a handful of unpredictable switches in style and register (e.g. 'to summarize our tale: we need a *fuck*', 715), and some eye-catching compound-words (e.g. *ō spermagoraiolekitholachanopōlides*, 'you market-place-breed-of-porridge-and-vegetable-saleswomen,   457), the verbal pyrotechnics found in other plays are simply thinner on the ground. What *Lysistrata* offers by way of compensation, however, is a series of more-rather-than-less tightly characterized figures, including a central character whose idiom, for all its flourishes, is arguably more consistent and true-to-life than that of any other protagonist in Aristophanes' fifth-century BCE comedies. Appropriately for a play built around a battle of the sexes, there is also a gendered dimension to the language used by men and women in *Lysistrata*, as we shall see, with key differences in the ways in which the two sexes communicate.

Once we take out of the equation 'marked' language – such as high-flown words and phrases borrowed from tragedy and the occasional technical expression – the default idiom of Aristophanes' comedies turns out to be the everyday language of contemporary Athens, making his plays a particularly rich resource for reconstructing Attic Greek as spoken in the middle of the classical era.[14] The text of *Lysistrata* can therefore provide a useful introduction of the idiosyncrasies of this dialect, such as the use of -*tt*- and -*rr*- by classical Athenians where speakers of most other Greek dialects would have used -*ss*- and -*rs*-, e.g. *diallattein*, 'to reconcile, make peace' (rather than *diallassein*, line 628) and *arren paidion*, 'baby *boy*' (rather than *arsen*, 748; see also Chapter 4 Section B on Spartan dialect). Also in abundance in *Lysistrata* are features of colloquial Attic which are either absent from or used sparingly in loftier genres, including the so-called 'deitic iota' – an -*i* freely tagged on the end of certain words as the verbal equivalent of pointing (e.g. *todi* 'this here thing . . ', 1008; *tasdi* 'these women here . . ', 244; *nuni*, 'right now', 1040).[15] A further feature of the spoken language is 'prodelision', namely the omission of a word's initial vowel sound, such as 's for *eis*, 'to' and *'pichein* for *epichein*, 'to pour in' (lines 2 and 197).[16] Notably, on a lexical level, the names of certain everyday objects are preserved largely or only in comic texts, without which our knowledge of classical Greek vocabulary would be much the poorer: examples from *Lysistrata* include 'cheese-grater' (*turoknēstis*, 231–2) and 'dildo' (*olisbos*, 109). For all the light that comedy can shine on the speech world of classical Athens, however, it is important to bear in mind that Aristophanes' plays are nevertheless poetic texts, composed within a broader literary tradition which could also embrace elements of linguistic artificiality. On a thematic level, the play's animal and weaving imagery, for example, and its use of motifs such as fire, water and salvation, clearly mark *Lysistrata* out as an artistic creation (see Chapter 2 Sections C and D). And, on a more mundane level, Aristophanes occasionally displays linguistic conservatism, such as in his use of the outmoded dative plural endings -*oisi* and -*aisi* alongside the more standard endings -*ois* and -*ais*. These -*oisi* and -*aisi* endings are liberally scattered throughout the text of *Lysistrata* – used by speakers of both sexes, young and old – yet are likely to have been obsolete in spoken Attic for some considerable time.[17]

One way in which philologically minded scholars have used Aristophanes' plays – alongside other evidence – is as source material to investigate possible differences between male and female speech in classical Athens. *Lysistrata* is a key text for this project, since female characters speak 768 of the play's 1,321 lines, or 58.1 per cent of the total, the highest proportion of any surviving comedy.[18] Of course, the sociolinguistic 'evidence' that this play provides needs to be handled with caution – after all, this is a literary text composed by a man for an essentially male audience, so while any given characteristic of female speech identified by modern scholars *may* be true-to-life (encoded either consciously or subconsciously by Aristophanes), this is not necessarily the case. 'Gendered' elements might equally reflect Aristophanes' artistic aims for the play and/or simply replicate common misconceptions about women's speech in classical Athens (indeed, Aristophanes arguably captures certain prejudices about female speech, e.g. by having his male characters trivialize women's talk as 'chatter', *lalein*, at lines 356, 442 and 637). Working with these caveats, scholarly studies have nevertheless thrown up some interesting results. Oaths are strongly gendered, for example: while men swear by a whole variety of male gods, women tend to swear either 'By Zeus' or, failing that, by a goddess or goddesses (Myrrhine's oath 'By Apollo' at line 917 is therefore highly unusual).[19] In comedy women are only very rarely named in front of men to whom they are not married (Lysistrata is a rare exception here: see Chapter 3 Section A) and tend not to utter obscenities in the presence of men (see below). As Andreas Willi has shown, women in comedy are also far more likely than men to employ what linguists call 'positive politeness strategies', such as terms of endearment ('darling', 15), praise of other women's actions ('yours is much better idea', 76; 'another good idea', 180) and (positive) comments about other women's appearance ('sweet, sweet lady, what beauty you display!', 79). They commonly use 'negative politeness strategies', too, i.e. ways of communicating that look to avoid confrontation or making strong statements. These include polite requests ('would you be willing, if I could find a plan …?', 111) and litotes ('not a difficult job', 1112; 'not badly educated', 1127). Both positive and negative politeness strategies are particularly concentrated in the prologue of *Lysistrata*, where the women's exchanges show them to be co-operative, polite and respectful of one another. Yet, as might be expected, they are less in evidence when Lysistrata and her comrades are conversing with the Proboulos. Interestingly, a number of these politeness strategies are apparent in Cinesias' exchange with his wife, too, as he seeks to win her over in the seduction scene: 'o sweet, sweet Myrrhine baby' (872), 'won't you come back?' (899), 'won't you lie down?' (906); 'that's really excellent' (913) – though as his sexual frustration mounts, he increasingly uses more direct language ('Now lie down, you miserable woman . . .!', 948).

Perhaps one of the most striking features of *Lysistrata* for modern audiences is its generous use of primary obscenities – words such as 'cock' (*peos*, 124, 415), 'cunt' (*kusthos*, 1158), 'fuck' (*bineō*, 1092) and 'shit' ((*epi*)*chezō*, 441–2), which make direct and unambiguous reference to sexual organs, sexual acts and defecation. Outside comedy, primary obscenities were employed in only a limited set of contexts in ancient Greece, most notably in various religious cults and festivals connected with Demeter and Dionysus, where ritual abuse, *aischrologia*, seems to have played a role in diverting the envy of the gods and marking out festival time as something distinct from everyday life.[20] Old Comic plays – which were themselves performed in the context of festivals in honour of Dionysus, of course (see Chapter 1 Section D) – would have therefore represented a rare occasion for Athenians to hear obscene language voiced in a public arena. Somewhat typically for Old Comedy, *Lysistrata* provides a whole catalogue of metaphorical, euphemistic and slang expressions for body parts and sexual acts, once again providing a rich insight into classical Greek vocabulary. Terms such as 'apples' (*māla*, i.e. breasts, 155), 'man-bag' (*sakandros*, i.e. vagina, 824) and 'spleck' (*splekoō*, 'to have intercourse' 152; possibly onomatopoeic in origin) are just the tip of the iceberg.[21]

Obscenity is put to a wide variety of uses in *Lysistrata*. It adds comedy and shock value to Lysistrata's revelation of her plan ('we must refrain from – cock', *peos*, 124) and an element of earthy humour to the oath she makes the women swear ('No man . . . shall come near me with a hard-on', *estukōs*, 214–15: see also Section A above). It provides a vehicle for Cinesias to voice his growing sexual frustration during the seduction scene ('By Zeus, I don't need [a blanket] – I want to *fuck!*', *binein*, 934) and subsequently brings a harsh note of desperation to his wishful fantasy that a whirlwind might seize his wife and that 'she would fall back down again to earth . . . astride my rock-hard dick' (*psōlē*, 979). Obscenity also provides a suitably crude ending for Lysistrata's oracle, whose high-flown and allusive language – which casts the restless women as 'swallows' looking to flee from Athena's 'sacred temple' – eventually gives way to a blunt revelation (774–6):[22]

> if the swallows are divided and fly aloft on wings out of the hallowed temple, no longer will there be thought to be any bird whatever that's . . . such an utter butt-spreading slut! (*katapugōnesteron*).

Primary obscenities do not only add splashes of risqué colour to *Lysistrata*, but are also a flexible tool which Aristophanes uses to add texture to the characterization of men and women and to develop themes of power and submission. The old women's preparedness to stand up to men, for example, is neatly reinforced by the muscular warning dished out by one of Lysistrata's companions to the Proboulos, 'if you lay so much as a hand on her, you'll get such a thrashing you'll *shit* yourself!' (*epichesei*, 439–40). As noted above (Chapter 4 Section A), this is one of the few obscenities in surviving comedy uttered by a woman to a man to whom she is not married, a fact that explains the Proboulos' apparently incredulous reaction '"Shit" you say?' (441). Indeed, while women in Old Comedy use obscenities in front of other women (as they do in the prologue of *Lysistrata*), and men are 'quite uninhibited about using these words in the presence of women', women only rarely utter them in the presence of men.[23] Even Lysistrata, who is otherwise very outspoken and the character who utters the most obscenities in the play, nevertheless avoids using primary obscenities in front of men. Indeed, during the reconciliation scene, she instructively refers to the men's penises using the relatively mild term *sathē*, 'willy' or 'member' in her command to the sexually alluring Reconciliation, 'if [any of the men] doesn't give you his hand, lead him by the member' (1118–19). Significantly, then, Lysistrata is shown to be capable of adapting her rhetorical strategies to suit her male audience – just as she also panders to them by producing Reconciliation in the first place and by prefacing her speech with a conventional piece of female rhetoric borrowed from tragedy: 'I may be a woman, but I do have a mind …' (1124; probably taken from Euripides' lost tragedy, *Melanippe the Wise*).[24] While Lysistrata's modified and restrained language accompanies her increased hold over the men, the continued use of obscenity by the younger men in the latter half of the play – interspersed with various slang terms for sexual organs – echoes and extends the sense of sexual desperation first articulated by Cinesias in the seduction scene ('Why, you wretch, you've got a hard-on!', *estukas*, 989; 'If someone doesn't reconcile us soon, there's nothing for it: we'll be fucking Cleisthenes!', *binēsomen*, 1091–2), with obscenity further employed in the reconciliation scene to underline the men's preoccupation with their sexual desires as they gaze at Reconciliation's body (e.g. 'I've never seen a more beautiful cunt', *kusthos*, 1158). Once peace has been made, however, all obscenities and references to the sexual realm melt away, leaving the celebratory scenes at the end of the play obscenity-free.

One group of words that deserve special mention for the gendered significance they assume in this play are those cognate with *philia*, 'friendship', 'affection', or 'alliance', and *philos*, 'friend', 'ally', 'dear', beloved', since these are strongly associated with female unity and the women's campaign. Women commonly use *phil-* words when addressing each other ('my dear Spartan friend' (*philē*), 140; 'Oh my dearest (*philtatē*), you're the only real woman here', 145) and also describe themselves as one another's 'friends' on more than one occasion ('Only your fair share, my friend!', *ō philē*, 238; 'Tell thy friends', *philais*, 712), but the men of *Lysistrata* never address or refer to each other in this way. Men are occasionally referred to as *philoi* ('friends') by women, however. Cinesias is twice addressed teasingly as 'dearest'/'darling' (*philtate*) during the seduction scene – first by Lysistrata (853), and then later when he is left in the lurch by Myrrhine with the words 'Do make sure you vote for peace, dearest' (950–1). And one man is even endorsed as a true 'friend' of the chorus of old women, namely the man-hating Timon, whom they describe as 'most friendly to women' (*philtatos*, line 820). The only other example of a male *philos* comes in the course of Lysistrata's wool metaphor where she suggests extending citizen rights to various social groups both inside and outside Athens, including 'any foreigner who's friendly (*philos*)' to the city (580). Instructively, then, this group of male *philoi* are something distinct from the warring Athenian and Spartan citizens who populate the play.[25]

Of particular interest is the way in which the verb *phileō*, 'I love', is used in *Lysistrata*. Notably, a woman can be credited with 'loving' a man (905–6):

Myrrhine   I won't say that I don't love (*phileō*) you.

Cinesias   You love (*phileis*) me? Then, why not lie down, Myrrhine sweetie?

Women 'kiss' others, too – also signalled by the verb *phileō* in Greek (e.g. 890 and 1036). But men are never the subject of the active verb *phileō*: unlike the women, then, they neither 'love' nor 'kiss'.[26] Indeed, while Myrrhine, as a woman, can claim to 'love' her husband, Cinesias, as a man, is spoken of as capable merely of *being* loved (870–1):

Myrrhine   I love him (*phileō*), I love him (*phileō*), but he doesn't want to be loved (*phileisthai*) by me.

Philia, then, is a concept closely linked to the female sphere and the campaign for peace – an idea which is reinforced by the fact that the younger women seal their pact over a 'cup of friendliness' (*kulix philotēsia*, 203), and by the women's chorus leader's description of her fellow older women as possessing 'patriotic (*philopolis*, lit. 'city-loving) valour' (546). But this is not to say that *philia* is an emotion completely absent from the world of men in *Lysistrata*. Towards the end of the play, the Spartan prays in his song that 'there may always be friendship (*philia*) in abundance thanks to our treaty' (1266–9). Crucially, then, with peace in prospect, and once the men are united in cause with the women, *philia* becomes a concept that is applicable to the male sphere, too.

(c) *Lysistrata*'s comic logic: Fantasy, discontinuity and plot

Compared with other plays of Aristophanes, *Lysistrata* is both tightly plotted and relatively sparing in its use of fantastic and far-fetched plotlines. Whereas the central character of *Peace*, the farmer Trygaeus, flies up to heaven on a giant dung beetle, and in *Frogs* Dionysus and his slave, Xanthias, journey to the Underworld, the entire action of *Lysistrata* takes place in contemporary Athens, and the two main components of the comic heroine's scheme – the sex strike and the women's seizure of the Acropolis – are at least *theoretically* possible in a way that riding to the gods' on an oversized arthropod and travelling to Hades are not. Tellingly, commentators on *Peace* and *Frogs* rarely spend much time outlining the ways in which the plotlines of these plays are unrealistic, yet the same cannot be said of *Lysistrata*.

Arguably, this is not only because the play's fantastic elements are deemed less outlandish by scholars than those of other comedies, but also because they are woven so skilfully into the fabric of the plot and emerge so effortlessly from the everyday, contemporary detail in which the play abounds as to make them seem almost plausible. As Alan Beale succinctly puts it, in *Lysistrata* 'things may happen in unexpected ways, yet in the context of the play [they] seem "quite natural"'.[27]

It is the sex-strike plot which is most often singled out for its numerous implausible elements. The scheme relies on the fact that all the men who are fighting the war are not only married (and are therefore able to be deprived of sex with their wives), but also have no other available sexual outlets outside wedlock. As many scholars have noted, unlike their real-life counterparts, neither sex with prostitutes nor with other males seems to be an option for *Lysistrata*'s men, who even appear to be incapable of masturbating![28] Given the men's long absences from home, as reported by the women in the prologue, it is also unclear why abstention from sex has not caused a problem for them before (lines 102–6).[29]

> **Calonice**   My husband . . . has been away for five months on the Thracian Coast . . . .
>
> **Myrrhine**   And mine's been away for seven whole months at Pylos.
>
> **Lampito**   And *mine*, even if he does ever come back from active service, straps his shield-band onto his arm again and goes flying off.

Conveniently for the plot of the play, however, Myrhhine's husband, Cinesias – as well as other men, it transpires – returns home just at the right moment for the sex strike to have maximum impact. In the latter half of the play, the effects of the strike are clearly visible in the permanent, swollen erections of the younger men – not only an implausible physical symptom in itself, but one that apparently afflicts them after just six days of enforced sexual abstinence (at line 881, Cinesias mentions this as the period of time for which Myrrhine has been absent from the house).

And what of the resolution of the sex-strike plot? The reconciliation scene is the part of the play where fantastic elements are at their most pronounced, since here are to be found the beguiling figure of Reconciliation herself – an abstract concept in female form – as well as the improbable peace settlement that Lysistrata brokers between the warring sides in just a few short minutes. Following this scene, the ithyphallic Athenian and Spartan men pile into the Acropolis to attend a drunken feast and gradually emerge some twenty-eight lines later, presumably now portrayed in a non-aroused state, the actors now sporting the traditional dangling phalluses more typical of comedy (lines 1188 and 1216). If the men's erections have subsided, is the audience meant to think that the husbands and wives have already paired up and satisfied their sexual desires as part of this celebration? The script is entirely silent on this point: the Athenian's report of the party (*sumposion*, 1225) centres instead on the charm of the Spartans, the cleverness of the Athenian attendees and the positive benefits that the consumption of alcohol can bring to inter-state relations (1226–38). Rather than seeing sex as an issue that Aristophanes has failed to address, however, it is no doubt more productive to view this passage as part of a broader pattern throughout the play of Aristophanes choosing to put an end to a given episode or plotline and to move the action quickly on by skilfully shifting the focus of attention. The result of this particular shift is that the men's need for sexual satisfaction, which was of such prime importance until just a few moments before, is now forgotten about and passed over, with the introduction of new topics of conversation helping to distract attention away from any loose threads left dangling in the plot.

There are many other sudden shifts in *Lysistrata* – not just in the focus of interest or topic of conversation, but also in place and time. As is often noted, the sex-strike plot, introduced so teasingly in the prologue, is all but forgotten about between lines 240 and 705 of the play, when the women's seizure and defence of the Acropolis take centre stage.[30] This rapid change of focus is brought about by Lampito's question to Lysistrata, 'What was that shout for?' (240), which allows the women's conversation to turn to the other component of Lysistrata's scheme – the taking of the Acropolis by the older women – and for the prologue to be brought to an end, with Lampito rapidly dispatched back to Sparta to 'arrange everything' there (243). Here, another important shift occurs, too, since the stage building which Lysistrata and the other women now enter seamlessly becomes the Acropolis, having formerly represented an anonymous Athenian house from which Calonice (and possibly Lysistrata, too, before her) emerged at the beginning of the play (See Chapter 2 Section B). A sudden shift in subject matter is a technique that Aristophanes uses to bring other episodes in the play to a close as well. For instance, the women's attempts to escape from the Acropolis are abruptly ended by Lysistrata when she produces an oracle predicting victory for the women; this in turn provides convenient grounds for them all to persist with the sex strike and return to the citadel ('So, let us not give up now despite our hardships; rather, let's go inside. For it would be a shameful thing, dearest friends, to betray the oracle!': lines 778–80). Similarly, the women's sudden decision to dress the Proboulos as a corpse brings the long Magistrate episode to an end by providing a useful pretext for his departure ('Really, is it not shocking that I should be treated like this? By Zeus, I'm going straight to the Magistrates (Probouloi) to show myself just as I am!' 608–10). In such instances the chain of logical cause and effect in the play can appear quite weak, resulting in a plot which at times can be better characterized as sequential (one thing after another) rather than strictly consequential (one thing because of another).[31] The play contains some unsignalled shifts in time, too. As mentioned above, it is only at line 881, when Cinesias casually states that it is six days since his wife abandoned him for the Acropolis, that we learn that significant time has passed since the sex strike began. And in the final scene the drunken feast and celebrations on the Acropolis are noticeably telescoped: the Athenian's description of the charm of the Spartans and cleverness of his own fellow citizens, plus the clear implication that there has been extensive drinking, hardly tally with the short period of stage time which has elapsed since the party began – as little as a couple of minutes, perhaps, while the chorus sings a short pair of humorous odes (1189–1215).

So, Aristophanes' mode of storytelling is capable of embracing not just fantasy and inconsistency, but also sudden shifts in focus, place and time – not that these elements are as prominent in *Lysistrata* as they are in many of his other fifth-century BCE plays.[32] What his work also embraces are shifts in characterization – a phenomenon which Michael Silk has termed 'recreativity', i.e. the ability that some figures in Aristophanes display to 're-create' themselves, typically through sudden and drastic changes in their persona, behaviour and/or the language they use.[33] Again, other plays provide more notable examples, but 'recreativity' can certainly be observed in the chorus(es) of *Lysistrata* who, despite being characterized relatively consistently as old men and old women, occasionally switch to the persona of chorus members in a play, addressing the audience directly ('Here we begin, all you citizens, to give the city some good advice . . .', 638–9). What is more, the light-hearted odes they deliver as a unified chorus towards the end of the play, again preceded by a short address to the audience (1043–6), also mark a significant change in the way they communicate. In both these jaunty songs they make a generous offer to the spectators – which each time turns out to be too good to be true (1043–71; 1188–1215):

Anyone who borrows money from us now will no longer have to pay it back – if he's had it!

So, come to my place today … you can walk in, no need to ask permission … just proceed boldly ahead in as if into your own home, because the door will be – shut!

There is little in the earlier characterization of the semi-choruses to hint at the cheery and mischievous new persona they display here, but in Aristophanic comedy, 'discontinuity' and 'stylistic switches' (to borrow Silk's terms) are not at all uncommon, especially in the case of choruses, whose identities are often changeable.[34] It is perhaps worth adding that, as with the other shifts noted above, reinventing the chorus as a vehicle for delivering upbeat, cheeky odes once again allows Aristophanes to drive the plot efficiently forwards, this time by signalling a change in theme and emotional direction as the play moves towards its celebratory conclusion.

Lysistrata in the Modern World

(a) Introduction

Lysistrata is that rare thing: an ancient comedy that has travelled beyond the confines of libraries, classrooms and lecture halls and found a niche for itself in the modern world. It has been performed countless times in theatres in the UK, the United States and beyond, even playing to sell-out audiences on Broadway. It has also been adapted as a piece of musical theatre and inspired more than one big budget film. Underpinning *Lysistrata*'s appeal is no doubt its status as a classical Greek text, combined with its risqué, attention-grabbing plotline: this is a play that allows audiences to have their culture and their dirty jokes, too. But equally important is the play's ability to provide an attractive jumping off point for the exploration of issues perceived as important in modern eras, such as: sex, sexuality and the limits of social decency; the place of women in society; popular protest; and the struggle for peace. It is the story of these interweaving strands of *Lysistrata*'s reception history from the nineteenth to the twenty-first centuries that this chapter will aim to tell.

Reception Studies – that is to say, the study of the ways in which a play like *Lysistrata* has been 'received', i.e. translated, adapted, understood and (re)performed in different cultural contexts – has gone from something of a niche pursuit amongst classical scholars in the 1980s and 1990s to a mainstream part of what it means to have a rounded understanding of an ancient text or object. On the one hand, reception can shed interesting light on the social history of a text's receiving cultures. In the case of *Lysistrata*, for example, studying the modern reception of the play provides a distinctive lens through which to view changing social attitudes towards women, sex and obscenity in recent historical periods and different cultural contexts. On the other hand, examining the play's reception history can reveal the wealth of different perspectives that translators, writers, directors and the public more broadly have brought to the play, thereby allowing us to see potentialities of the text that we might not otherwise spot. The ability for the play to be successfully adapted and staged *both* to titillate all-male audiences *and*, alternatively, to support feminist causes is certainly thought-provoking, for example (see Sections C and E below). Importantly, too, a long view of *Lysistrata*'s reception history can help us to identify and articulate the nature of our own culturally contingent viewpoint. Modern readers, translators, directors and audiences are not neutral observers, after all. We, too, bring our own assumptions and cultural baggage to the play which in turn shapes the way that we view and seek to understand *Lysistrata*. In short, an understanding of *Lysistrata*'s reception history allows us to be better students of the play.

Given the popularity – and notoriety – of *Lysistrata* in the twentieth and twenty-first centuries, what is perhaps surprising is the extent to which it was passed over by scholars and translators in the centuries before, reduced to something of an 'also ran' when compared with other Aristophanic plays. When the first modern edition of Aristophanes' plays appeared in Italy in 1498, for example, the ancient Greek texts of nine out of the eleven surviving Aristophanic plays were duly published, but *Lysistrata* (along with *Thesmophoriazusae*) would have to wait until 1515–16 to appear in print. In a similar vein, when it comes to tracing the history of published translations of Aristophanes' plays in various European languages – as well as their occasional adaptation for the stage – *Wealth* and *Clouds* often led the way, while *Lysistrata* was characteristically a late arrival on the scene. In England, for instance, an updated adaptation of *Wealth* (*The World's*

Idol; or, Plutus the God of Wealth) was staged in London in 1651 and English translations of selected passages from *Clouds* first appeared in print in 1655 (full translations of both plays subsequently appeared in 1659 and 1715 respectively, eventually joined by *Frogs* in 1785). The British public had to wait until 1837, however, for a (severely expurgated) version of *Lysistrata* to appear – in a volume by C. A. Wheelwright containing all eleven plays – and its first recorded public performance in the English-speaking world would not take place until 1910, in a production staged in London to support the campaign for votes for women (see Section C below). Of course, much of the explanation for this historic reluctance to engage with *Lysistrata* can be accounted for by the play's overtly sexual content, something which has continued to make the play both appealing *and* problematic for translators, adaptors, directors and audiences of the play in more recent times, as we shall see.

Sex may loom large in *Lysistrata*'s reception history in the twentieth and twenty-first centuries, but so do its links with feminism and pacificism – associations which might also be thought of as problematic, albeit for a very different set of reasons. The issue here is that the connection of *Lysistrata* with both these causes arguably represents a misreading of Aristophanes' play. After all, as Alan Sommerstein has shown, *Lysistrata* is far from a 'pacifist' play in the strict sense of the word: its heroine may be interested in bringing the Peloponnesian War to an end, but she is neither opposed to war in general nor does she shy away from violent means to achieve her aims.[1] Similarly, a number of factors stand in the way of *Lysistrata* being read as a wholeheartedly proto-feminist play. Needless to say, the young women of Aristophanes' play are hardly feminist role models (see Chapter 1 Section D), and while Lysistrata is certainly a strong woman who ultimately succeeds in her goals, what she also achieves in securing peace is a return to the traditional social structures that prevailed before the war (men will again govern the city and head up its households, while women will resume their conventional domestic and sexual roles). However, if viewing *Lysistrata* in a pacifist or feminist light is to misrepresent the original play, this might nevertheless be seen as a 'productive misreading', to use Martin Revermann's memorable phrase: a way of approaching the play which has allowed modern writers, directors and audiences 'to interact with [*Lysistrata*] in ways that are meaningful to them'.[2] As Revermann goes on to say, these arguably inauthentic ways of understanding the play often serve to make the text more relevant for modern audiences and can therefore be viewed as 'a necessary part of making the ancient text "ours"'.[3]

The rest of this chapter seeks to trace the reception history of *Lysistrata* from the nineteenth to the twenty-first centuries, exploring how the play has been translated, adapted, staged and reconfigured for new audiences. The main focus is on the English-speaking world – in particular, the UK and the United States, where *Lysistrata* has generally enjoyed its largest audiences – but other linguistic and cultural traditions are also touched on along the way with a view to tracing lines of influence, exploring points of comparison, and conveying something of the impact and influence that the play has enjoyed globally. The chapter is structured broadly chronologically, beginning in Victorian Britain and ending with examples of *Lysistrata*'s reception in twenty-first century America. Yet its various sections also dwell on key themes associated with the different eras discussed: sex and prudishness, titillation and feminism, war and peace, political protest and social conformity – these all feature strongly in the story of *Lysistrata*'s reception, and readers interested in particular eras or topics can use the section titles to locate the material of most relevance to them. Finally, the conclusion of the chapter aims to bring the various threads of the discussion together and to consider what future generations might make of Aristophanes' play.

(b) Translating *Lysistrata* in Victorian Britain:
Skirting around obscenity

Prior to 1800, only three of Aristophanes' plays had been translated into English (see Section A), making him one of the least translated of major classical authors. All that was about to change, however, with the nineteenth century representing something of a boom in Aristophanic translation in Britain. While plays like *Frogs* and *Clouds* were firm favourites with Victorian translators, however, 'women' plays such as *Lysistrata* were rarely touched on. Indeed, along with *Thesmophoriazusae* and *Peace*, *Lysistrata* was one of the last three of Aristophanes' plays to be published in an English translation, forced to wait until 1837 before it could be enjoyed by an anglophone readership. It was in this year that *Lysistrata* eventually appeared, rendered in jaunty free verse, in *The Comedies of Aristophanes* by C. A. Wheelwright, the first English-language volume to contain all eleven surviving comedies. As might be expected, strong language and scurrilous references were generally avoided both in Wheelwright's and other pre-twentieth-century versions of Aristophanes' plays, with Victorian translators typically conforming to contemporary notions of taste and decency by erasing all obscenities and toning down their indelicacies. And so *Lysistrata*'s women are asked not to give up 'cock' (*peos*) in this 1837 version, but rather to 'spare the conjugal embrace' (line 131 of the translation; 124 of the Greek) and references to lovers and dildos (lines 107 and 109) are excised – along with the entirety of the seduction and reconciliation scenes (lines 828–1215). Given this reluctance of translators to engage with sexual material, it perhaps comes as no surprise that *Lysistrata* remained stubbornly unpopular for a number of decades after Wheelwright's translation was published. While many of Aristophanes' plays could be read in a variety of English translations by the end of the nineteenth century, in 1900 English speakers wishing to read *Lysistrata* had only two further volumes to choose from: those of B. B. Rogers (1878) and Samuel Smith (1896).

Benjamin Bickley Rogers is something of a giant in the world of Aristophanic translation. A practising barrister and amateur classicist, Rogers published his first Aristophanic translation, *Clouds*, in 1852, eventually going on to produce editions of all eleven extant plays. Distinctive for their rich use of language (such as high-register, poetic vocabulary and colloquial archaisms) as well as the often complex versification Rogers employs for the play's lyric passages in an attempt to imitate the rhythms of the original Greek, Rogers' versions of the comedies went on to be published in numerous editions in the twentieth century. Indeed, they established themselves as 'the one and only version of Aristophanes' for anglophone readers for many years to come, not least because they went on to form the basis of the Loeb Classical Library editions of Aristophanes (only superseded by Henderson's Loeb editions, which came out between 1998 and 2002).[4] Rogers' translation of *Lysistrata* was first published as *The Revolt of the Women* in 1878 and subsequently formed the basis of a scholarly edition of the play with additional material published in 1911. In his version of the play – billed on the title page of the 1878 edition as 'a free translation' – obscene references are either avoided, replaced by euphemisms, or jettisoned entirely; or as a reviewer of the 1911 version put it, '[m]any things that stand unashamed in the Greek are decently clad or put away in the English'.[5] In fact, Rogers chose to leave out some of the play's more risqué parts altogether: for the Loeb reprint – a series which provides a facing-page English translation to accompany the original text – the scurrilous passages of *Lysistrata* which Rogers had omitted were anonymously translated and reinserted.[6]

A flavour of Roger's translation can be gained from the following extract taken from the prologue of the play, where Lysistrata, Lampito and Calonice deliver some risqué *double entendres* about the Boeotian and Corinthian women who have just arrived in Athens: the former is said to have 'a fine low-lying region' with shoots of pennyroyal neatly plucked out (88–9: a reference to her pubic region) and the latter to have a 'noble' appearance (91) – which Calonice says that she displays 'up here and down there', no doubt pointing to her breasts, belly and/ or buttocks (90–2). Not only is Rogers' avoidance of scurrility in evidence in this passage, but also his Victorian sensibilities when it comes to his choice of vocabulary ('whence', 'damsel' and 'ay'). Notable, too, are both his attempt to reflect something of the versification of the original and his decision (taken by some later British translators, too) to render Lampito's distinctive Spartan dialect in a form of Scots English (*Lysistrata* 85–92).[7]

> **Lys**.   And who's this other damsel? whence comes she?
> **Lamp**.   Ane deputation frae Bœoty, comin'
> To sit amang you.   **Lys**.   Ah, from fair Bœotia,
> The land of plains !   **Cal**.   A very lovely land.
> Well cropped, and trimmed, and spruce with penny-royal.
> **Lys**.   And who's the next ? **Lamp**. A bonnie burdie she.
> She's a Corinthian lassie.   **Lys**.   Ay, by Zeus,
> And so she is. A bonnie lass, indeed.

If bowdlerization was the rule when it came to translating Aristophanes in the nineteenth century, then the exception that proves it is a famous edition of *Lysistrata* published in 1896, with its suggestive text by an anonymous translator (since identified as Samuel Smith) and its erotic illustrations by Aubrey Beardsley. Edith Hall comments that this privately published edition of the play – arguably the most notorious from any era – is 'important as the first faithful and unexpurgated translation of *Lysistrata* into the English language', though alongside the 'shaven coyntes' (line 151) and footnotes about dildos and sexual positions, the translator still opts to translate *peos* as 'penis' and to render Lysistrata's 'we need a fuck' as 'we are dying with

desire!' (lines 124 and 715).[8] Beardsley's eight pen-and-ink drawings
for this volume are particularly risqué, portraying naked women,
giant erect penises, and acts of female flatulence and masturbation
(see, for example, Figure 5.1). Beardsley's conversion to Catholicism
ahead of his death in 1898, at the age of just twenty-five, led him to
write to his publisher begging him to 'destroy *all* copies of *Lysistrata*
and ... *all* obscene drawings', but the work survived to be reprinted
(often in expurgated form) several times in the twentieth century and

Figure 5.1 'Lysistrata Shielding her Coynte' by Aubrey Beardsley (1896).

beyond. The volume was to remain controversial for many years to come, however, and as late as 1966 copies of the book were confiscated by authorities in the UK under the Obscene Publications acts.[9] This particular *Lysistrata* was self-consciously counter-cultural in its conception, but its initial publication and continued circulation in the twentieth century betrays a clear interest, among some readers at least, in exploring the sexuality and obscenity to be found Aristophanes' play.

(c) Sexy, sexist and suffragette *Lysistratas*: Early adaptations on the European stage

While in Victorian Britain *Lysistrata* was variously cleaned up for a public readership, sexed up for strictly private consumption or simply ignored, the play was to enjoy a somewhat different fate across the English Channel. In the theatre scene of fin-de-siècle Paris, female figures from Greek myth and history, such as Aphrodite, Helen of Troy or famous *hetairai* ('courtesans') regularly featured in popular shows and cabarets which, in the words of one scholar, 'objectified mythical or legendary women for the sake of male voyeuristic pleasure'.[10] Lysistrata was a particularly prominent figure in this tradition of classically themed revue, largely thanks to a version of *Lysistrata* written by Maurice Donnay which premiered at the Grand-Théâtre in Paris in 1892.[11] A composer for, and performer at, the celebrated *le chat noir* cabaret in Montmartre, Donnay radically reworked the play, eroticizing it in the style of a contemporary French revue (for example by introducing a classical courtesan figure in the form of Salabaccho) and reconfiguring the script as a comedy of sexual manners and marital duplicity. A striking feature of this version is that Lysistrata – who is married in this play to an Athenian named Lycon – breaks the oath of sexual abstinence she has sworn by sleeping with her lover, Agathos, and in so doing symbolically overturns a statue of Artemis in the temple where the tryst takes place. Donnay's *Lysistrata* was both popular and influential, spawning further productions and imitations of the play both in Paris and beyond.[12]

The reception of *Lysistrata* in early twentieth-century Greece (as well as the other 'women' plays of Aristophanes, *Thesmophoriazusae* and *Assemblywomen*) was influenced by this Parisian tradition, too. The first Modern Greek production of *Lysistrata* was staged in 1905 at the Municipal Theatre in Athens in a version by the prolific translator and playwright Polyvios Demetrakopoulos which, in Gonda Van Steen's words, was 'infused with ... jokes, obscenities, sociopolitical anachronisms and antifeminist satire'.[13] Importantly, Demetrakopoulos' text was later adapted and reperformed in ways that both drew on Parisian traditions and reconfigured the play for contemporary Athenian audiences. Female spectators were forbidden from attending these risqué spectacles, which were performed by all-male casts as part of a broader tradition of erotic and transvestite cabaret in contemporary Athens (sometimes advertised as 'soireé noire'), with the lead roles taken by established transvestite actors ('imitateurs' or 'metamorphotes').[14] The appeal of *Lysistrata* was evidently strong, with versions of the play continuing to be performed in Athens throughout the early decades of the twentieth century, providing all-male audiences with a distinctively sexist and voyeuristic form of entertainment, only loosely based on Aristophanes' play.

Back in the UK, the appetite – and indeed the stomach – for *Lysistrata* was much less in evidence in the early twentieth century, where the play's first English-language performance catered for a very different audience from those found in the cabarets of Paris and Athens. Chosen for its potential to bolster the cause of women's suffrage, *Lysistrata* was first staged in the UK at the Little Theatre in the Adelphi, London, in 1910. The theatre leaseholder, Gertrude

Kingston, was an experienced actor of Greek drama and took the title role in the play, performed in a free translation by Laurence Housman (the brother of the poet A. E. Housman) who was a founder member of the Men's League for Women's Suffrage in England (the script even included a number of suffrage jokes). As Edith Hall notes, 'the London theatregoing public had become accustomed to women of the theatre, who had long been prominent voices in support of female suffrage, performing in ancient Greek dramas that gave women shocking things to do and say', and so in one sense this production of *Lysistrata* was not revolutionary. Rather, it sat firmly within – yet, also served to extend – a tradition of Greek drama being used as a vehicle to support the case for votes for women.[15] The heavy bowdlerization of the text gave one reviewer the pretext to dismiss the production as a 'tame and school-girlish affair',[16] but the significance of this version of *Lysistrata* clearly went beyond its (lack of) risqué humour. Housman's translation of the play was used for the first performance of *Lysistrata* in the United States, too, where it was staged in support of the cause of women's suffrage at the Cleveland College for Women in 1914.[17]

Lysistrata was not destined to become a popular play in the UK for some time. It was, however, staged in Cambridge in 1931 using the translation by Arthur Way,[18] and also performed as a ballet, *Lysistrata* or *The Strike of Wives*, at the Mercury Theatre in London in 1932.[19] It was not until 1957–8 that the play was brought to wider public attention under Minos Volanakes' direction at the Royal Court (using the translation by Dudley Fitts), a production which subsequently transferred to the Duke of York's Theatre in London's West End.[20] The play, although not universally praised by reviewers, was a big hit with the public. All the while, of course, British productions had to be careful to stay the right side of the censor, a rare exception being an unexpurgated version of an adaptation of *Lysistrata*, penned by Reginald Beckwith and Andrew Cruikshank,[21] which was produced in 1935 at Norman Marshall's Gate Theatre – one of a small number of theatres in London which operated as 'theatre clubs' in order to avoid censorship by the Lord Chamberlain. It was only in 1968 that the Theatres Act would finally put an end to formal censorship on the British stage.

(d) Embracing and avoiding controversy in mid-twentieth-century America: Broadway, Hollywood and the censor

The reception history of Aristophanes on the US stage in the first half of the twentieth century is somewhat dominated by Bel Geddes' *Lysistrata*, which enjoyed considerable commercial success on Broadway in 1930–1. This play was itself influenced by a notable Moscow Art Theatre production of *Lysistrata*, directed by Nemirovich-Danchenko and first performed in Moscow in 1923. This Russian, musical version of *Lysistrata* had garnered considerable public interest and critical acclaim when it was brought to the United States in 1925–6.[22] The man who had co-translated the Russian script of the play into English (which was made available to American audience members) was Gilbert Seldes, a theatre critic, author and book reviewer, with a particular interest in popular entertainment. Seeing the potential of the play to appeal to contemporary audiences, Seldes went on to write his own American version of *Lysistrata*, into which he injected modern, popular elements such as song, dance, farce and burlesque.[23] It was Seldes' version, directed by Bel Geddes, which became a big Broadway hit, running for 256 performances at the Forty-Fourth Street Theatre, New York, and spawning further productions which toured throughout the United States.[24]

One of the more noteworthy elements of Seldes' version of *Lysistrata* is the way in which the female roles are reworked. In contrast to Lysistrata and the older women, who are deeply earnest in their concern about the war and other social issues, the younger women are frivolous, ineffectual and even less able to meet the challenge of the sex strike than the women in Aristophanes' original play. They engage in extensive squabbling about Lysistrata's plan, and, during the swearing of the oath, two of the women even become hysterical. The themes of sexual temptation and adultery are also dwelt on at length in the play. Not only is the seduction scene expanded to take in three more couples, but Calonice (or Kalonika, as her name is spelt in the text) also appears onstage at one point in a dishevelled state, having apparently given in to temptation. Interestingly, too, in common with a number of adaptations of the play, Lysistrata – a young woman in Seldes' version – is given a husband, Lycon, whom we meet briefly towards the end of the play.[25] As scholars have noted in their discussions of the production, when it came to costumes, Bel Geddes' attentions were firmly on the young stars of his production – particularly the women, whose sexual appeal he sought to maximize by having them 'dressed in transparent drapery' that provided 'ample peeks at the bodies beneath'.[26] Miriam Hopkins, for example, who played Kalonika in the show, was costumed in flowing chiffon that revealed her bare breasts beneath (see Figure 5.2).

This engagement with sexuality and sexiness required some careful handling if *Lysistrata* was to stay on the right side of the censors. As Marina Kotzamani records, the authorities in Philadelphia, where the play was first staged before transferring to New York, did cut some lines and threatened to cut more, leading the play's producers to take pre-emptive action in New York by defending the play's morality in a note in the programme.[27] Not that this entirely allayed the authorities' concerns; and when the play eventually opened in New York, police were stationed in the auditorium to ensure that the production kept on the right side of decency. As Seldes remarks in his foreword to the visually stunning 1934 edition of the play, which contains a series of etchings by Pablo Picasso, the censor did put a stop to one performance

Figure 5.2 Miriam Hopkins as Kalonika in Norman Bel Geddes' 1930–1 Broadway production of *Lysistrata*.

in Los Angeles, however, where police stormed the stage, arresting fifty-three members of the cast. Indeed, a warrant was even drawn up for the arrest of Aristophanes himself.[28]

This was not to be the last time that *Lysistrata* had brushes with the censors in the United States. For example, a much-discussed 1936 adaptation of the play *Lysistrata of Aristophanes: An African Version*, performed by an all-black cast in Seattle, Washington, sponsored by the Federal Theatre Project (an offshoot of Franklin D. Roosevelt's Works Progress Administration) was closed after only one

performance, allegedly for being 'indecent and bawdy'.[29] The charged
events surrounding this act of censorship seem to point to race
playing an important role, with a number of modern commentators
highlighting white anxieties about black female sexuality as one key
factor.[30] There is, however, also a strong tradition of *Lysistrata*
successfully avoiding censorship in mainstream theatres in the United
States. While the proven appeal and performability of the Seldes
version of the play no doubt accounts in large part for its wide use
in productions of the play in mid-century America, the fact that it
had previously survived its skirmishes with censorship must also
have made the play a reassuringly safe bet.[31] One noteworthy – if
short-lived – Broadway revival of Seldes' text was staged at the
Belasco Theatre in 1946, with an all-black cast that included a young
Sidney Poitier.

Of course, one way to sidestep issues of censorship altogether –
and to extend the appeal of the play to new audiences – is to adapt
Lysistrata in such a way as to avoid explicit references to the sexual
sphere. This was a tactic employed by Universal Studios' 1955 film *The
Second Greatest Sex*, a musical-comedy western very much in the
mould of the box-office smash *Oklahoma!* which was released earlier
that same year.[32] The action of the movie takes place in the Wild West
of the 1880s where – instead of a war – the menfolk of the district
abandon their women to engage in a petty squabble over which
town should be the county seat.[33] While the film certainly provided
physically attractive leading actors – in the form of Hollywood
favourite, Jeanne Crain, screen siren Mamie Van Doren, and the burly
George Nader – the script and lyrics were carefully crafted to be
family friendly. The sexuality of this 1950s *Lysistrata* lies very much
under the surface, confined within a series of figure-hugging dresses
and the occasional knowing line, both of which are largely the preserve
of the buxom blonde character, Birdie (played by Van Doren).[34]
Admiring Liza's wedding dress, for instance, she remarks: 'Oh, if I had

a white satin wedding dress, I'd never take it off! Well, hardly ever'. As one scholar observes, the film presents 'a deeply conservative feminine ideal' for women, with gender roles and expectations clearly defined.[35] Marriage is of central importance for the wholesome Liza – 'What good is a woman without a man? Answer me that if anybody can' – and her efforts to end the dispute are very much geared to restoring the domestic order which the men's conflict threatens to disrupt.

A further attempt to restyle Lysistrata as a sexually tame musical came in 1961. Destined for only a short run on Broadway, *The Happiest Girl in the World*, with lyrics by Yip Harburg, opened in April of that year at the Martin Beck Theatre only to close three months later. In this version, Lysistrata is involved in a peculiar love triangle with her husband, the Athenian general, Kinesias, and the goddess Diana. Interestingly, while Lysistrata is the show's title character – the 'happiest girl in the world', as she sings near the beginning of the play, because her husband has returned from war – she is not the show's protagonist. Rather, along with other mortals, Lysistrata is portrayed as a pawn of the gods Diana and Pluto (who have the two meatiest roles in this musical) rather than a forceful personality in her own right. Indeed, even the idea for a sex strike is sent to her by Diana in a dream.[36]

(e) *Lysistrata* hits the big time: Sex and sexual politics in the spotlight in the late twentieth and early twenty-first centuries

It is not just in Hollywood that there was interest in *Lysistrata* in the post-war decades. The play was staged in a variety of cultural settings in the 1950s and 1960s, where it often aroused both interest and opposition as a play which explored and tested the limits of public attitudes towards sexualized material. The BBC productions of

Lysistrata dating from this period are an interesting case in point, with a 1957 radio broadcast of the play paving the way for a television version in 1964, *Lysistrata; or Women on Strike*, starring Diane Cilento in the title role.[37] Although Patric Dickinson's version of the play had been severely trimmed for the TV version so that 'it did not offend the sensitive mass audience',[38] it still contained what one critic described as 'dirty jokes ... put over ... unblushingly by most of the cast'.[39] Responses to the broadcast were mixed, with some viewers finding the play 'full of cheek' and 'fun', others considering it 'disgusting and coarse'.[40] Greek comedy, with its veneer of classical 'respectability', provided a vehicle for artists and audiences to explore and push the boundaries of acceptability in other cultures, too. In her article 'Greek Drama in Rhodesia/Zimbabwe', for example, Jessie Maritz discusses a performance of *Lysistrata* which also took place in 1964 – this time in Sailsbury (modern-day Harare). In this production, the girls wore bikinis: a daring move, she notes, since these had been banned at public swimming baths four years earlier.[41]

The beginning of the 1960s and 1970s marked something of a turning point for *Lysistrata*, since it is at this point in time that its popularity on the English-speaking stage began to soar. The University of Oxford's *Archive of Performances of Greek and Roman Drama* records three productions of *Lysistrata* in the United States in the 1950s. This rises to seven in the 1960s and eight in the 1970s, with a number of these productions staged on US university campuses in response to the Vietnam War.[42] Following the 1980s, the popularity of the play surges once again: we find eleven productions in the United States in the 1990s and the same number in the UK, rising to sixteen in the United States and twenty in the UK in the 2000s.[43] The venues of these productions are significant, too. Alongside big budget productions – such as Peter Hall's 1993 *Lysistrata* staged at Liverpool Playhouse before transferring to London's Old Vic Theatre – we find numerous stagings of the play in regional theatres, in a wealth of universities, and by local amateur companies and even school groups. A 1986 Cambridge Greek Play production represented what was perhaps the first staging of the play in the original Greek since ancient times – soon to be followed by memorable original-language versions at King's College London in 1995 and a further Cambridge Greek Play production in 2016 (in a high-energy production directed by Helen Eastman, full of political satire, songs and silliness: see Figure 5.3). In short, *Lysistrata* hit the big time, achieving a reach and popularity that no other ancient comedy in modern times has even begun to rival.

So what is the attraction of Lysistrata to audiences and directors? If marketing material is anything to go by, then sex has regularly been a key ingredient of selling a production to potential theatre-goers. At the mild end of the spectrum is the Actors of Dionysus' 2010 *Lysistrata*, billed in one newspaper as 'riotous, irreverent and very naughty'.[44] More provocatively, according to the website advertising the version

Figure 5.3 Still from the 2016 Cambridge Greek Play production of *Lysistrata*, featuring Natasha Cutler (centre) in the title role.

of the play staged at Stone on a Walk Theatre, Cincinnati, in 2015, 'You won't look at war the same again after *Lysistrata* shows you how hard the last few inches to peace can be'.[45] Reviewers, too, are often quick to emphasize the sexual themes of Aristophanes' play: 'All present and erect' was the headline of one review of Peter Hall's *Lysistrata*, staged in a translation by Ranjit Bolt.[46]

One way to trace changing attitudes towards Aristophanic sex and obscenity in the late twentieth and early twenty-first centuries is to examine how the obscene vocabulary in the plays is handled in the welter of translations that were published in this era. The most climactic obscenity of *Lysistrata*, the *peos* uttered by Lysistrata as she reveals what she is asking the women to give up, has changed from 'the joys of Love' in B. B. Rogers' translation (first published in 1878) to Doros Alastos' 'copulation and concubinage' (1953), Patric Dickinson's 'sleeping with them' (1957), Alan Sommerstein's 'sex' (1973) and 'cock and balls' (1990), Jeffrey Henderson's 'cock' (1996) and 'prick' (2000), Stephen Halliwell's 'prick' (1997), X. J. Kennedy's 'letting our husbands lay us' (1999), Sarah Ruden's 'penises' (2003), Paul Roche's *'phallus'* (2004), David Stuttard's 'sex' (2010), Michael Ewan's 'prick' (2011) and David Mulroy's 'PENISES' (2020).[47] While there is, then, a tendency for the translation of *peos* to become more direct over time, it is interesting how many translators choose to avoid outright obscenity when rendering the word. Greer and Willmott's paraphrase, 'Until our men see sense we simply refuse to fuck', which Lysistrata comically blurts out after a number of failed attempts at finding the right words, is something of an outlier (their version of *Lysistrata* was first staged in 1999 and published in 2011). Of course, much of the explanation here lies in the fact that translators have their own diverse objectives and sensibilities and are often aiming to appeal to particular audiences. As Halliwell notes, there are 'few [translators] who shirk nothing in this area'.[48]

Aristophanic 'naughtiness' may help to get bums on theatre seats, but it is also worth bearing in mind that even in the twenty-first century, obscene and sexual content still has the power to shock and offend. Jeffrey Henderson, for instance, calls the 'reluctance of performers to enact, and audiences to come out for "obscene" material' an 'occupational hazard' for theatre producers, citing the headline-grabbing case of the musical adaptation of *Lysistrata*, which was due to be staged in 2002 by the American Repertory Theater in Cambridge, Massachusetts, but was pulled during rehearsal for being 'too bawdy'.[49] Nor is it just obscene and sexual vocabulary that can be found challenging: the sexuality of Aristophanes' plays – with what Stephen Halliwell has described as their 'erotics of shamelessness' – can also find itself at odds with the contemporary sexual mores of the culture for which they are being translated or staged.[50]

Feminist critiques have long since exposed the 'masculinist' nature of Aristophanes' plays, with their misogynist stereotypes of women and their inclusion of what Bella Zweig has called 'mute, nude female characters' whose main function is to fulfil men's sexual needs.[51] So, what do modern directors do when faced with the challenge of staging the figure of an ostensibly nude, objectified woman, such as Reconciliation in *Lysistrata*? A common choice is to cast a man in this role and to exploit the comic potential of travesty acting at the same time as sidestepping some – if by no means all – of the uncomfortable gender politics with which the original play confronts them. Other directorial decisions are more radical, however. A 2010 staging of a scene from *Lysistrata* at East Carolina University followed the convention of using a male actor in a padded body suit to play the mute, nude character of Reconciliation, but then delivered a devastating twist. In an attempt to convey what the director, John Given, describes as 'the dramatic and thematic functions' of the original scene, namely 'the restabilization of [the] political world order and its gender roles', Lysistrata first ordered the actor playing

Reconciliation offstage, then stripped to reveal a modest slip, and proceeded to play the role of Reconciliation herself.[52] The strong female character at the heart of *Lysistrata* was thus reduced to a sexual object as she was groped and prodded by the Athenian and Spartan delegates. This staging was aimed not just at highlighting and heightening the act of objectification itself but also at stressing the consequences of the successful negotiation of peace with which the play ends: once the war ceases, the play's women surrender the power they previously exercised over men and return to their roles as subordinate housewives.

A different response to the 'masculinist' nature of Aristophanic sexual ethics is to produce an adaptation of the play with a feminist agenda, such as *Lysistrata: The Sex Strike*, a version penned by the feminist intellectual Germaine Greer, with additional material by the British playwright and theatre director Phil Willmott, and first performed in London in 1999. (Greer's interest in the play had originally been sparked some thirty years before, when she began working on a version of *Lysistrata* in response to the Vietnam War, an act of authorship which itself built on the tradition of anti-war stagings of the play in the 1960s and 1970s: see above.) Greer and Willmott remain faithful to the original structure of *Lysistrata* and preserve the backdrop of the Peloponnesian War, but modernize elements, too, setting the action of the play in a bathhouse (an all-male space that the women then infiltrate) and injecting the text with some outrageous crowd-pleasing humour (such as the Spartan women's chant: 'Spartan girls are fit and tough … We can take it hard and rough').[53] One reviewer of the production, staged at the Battersea Arts Theatre, called it 'as saucy and breezy as a seaside postcard'.[54] Yet this unashamedly commercial retelling of *Lysistrata* nevertheless packed some subtle feminist punches. When told that 'War is men's business,' for example, Lysistrata justifies her need to intervene with action (as well as words) by retorting:[55]

> I couldn't sit quietly any longer.... I couldn't sit there and do nothing
> while whole civilisations butchered each other. I believe in negotiating
> for peace. That's why I set up a peace treaty with the enemy who are as
> demoralised as we are ... Oh, with the women of course, just to make
> you understand that it's only the men who are at war. We women have
> never declared war on each other in any country ever in history.

Other feminist productions of *Lysistrata* have been more radical in their approach, none more so, perhaps, than the anarchic and experimental *Lysistrata Numbah!*, staged in New York in 1977 by Spiderwoman Theater. In her account of this production, Emily Klein records how the company's distinctive 'patchwork aesthetic' allowed the all-female cast to combine parody and clowning with scenes of violence and loss, all interspersed with often intimate stories taken from the actors' own lives (the show's content ranged from bungled dance routines through simulated masturbation to a personal account of abortion).[56] 'Too raunchy and slapstick to be feminist and too rough to be good theatre' – as one critic put it – *Lysistrata Numbah!* not only used *Lysistrata* as a springboard to launch a feminist critique of how little society had changed in the last 2,500 years, but also directed its biting satire at other targets, including contemporary feminism itself.[57]

(f) Lysistrata the pacificist

As mentioned in the introduction to this chapter, *Lysistrata* has a long history of being staged and adapted not only to promote feminist agendas, but also to support the pacificist cause. Indeed, one of the earliest productions in the United States of a *Lysistrata*-inspired play was George Cram Cook's *Athenian Women*, a self-consciously anti-war piece staged by his Provincetown Players in 1918.[58] For all its raunchiness, the Broadway *Lysistrata* of 1930–31, too – written when memories of the First World War were still relatively fresh – carried a strong anti-war message, with Seldes using evocative images to amplify the points that Lysistrata makes about the different ways in which men and women experience conflict.[59]

> We ... carry the child in our womb and stand at the threshold of death at the moment of bringing forth life. You sit in council chambers, and vote for war and send out your expeditionary forces. But the young men who die are the children we bore and nursed at our breast and gave our strength to – and our youth. When their bodies lie buried in strange ground, a part of us is buried there. That is our burden of war.

Greer's version of the play, *The Sex Strike*, evokes the horrors of modern warfare, too, namely the atrocities committed in conflicts such as the Vietnam War. These are drawn on by Greer when she puts into Myrrhine's mouth concerns about the dehumanizing effect that war can have on male combatants. During the seduction scene, she says to her husband:[60]

> I've been worrying about you since the day you left. I have terrible dreams of you ... running wild with the other soldiers, killing children and raping women like a maniac. I'm frightened that you've turned into a monster.

Greer's play does not just problematize war, however; it actively embraces a pacificist agenda, as we have seen. 'I believe in negotiating for peace,' says Lysistrata, and it is not just the continuation of the Peloponnesian War that she opposes (which is also the case in Aristophanes' play, of course) but war in any form. Importantly, too, when reflecting on the history of conflict in general, Lysistrata identifies war as something for which men alone have been responsible in the past: 'We women have never declared war on each other in any country ever in history.' Men are characterized as warmongers in Greer's play and women as peacemakers; pacifism and feminism are thus intertwined.

Perhaps the most famous anti-war adaptation of *Lysistrata* is *The Common Chorus* by the British playwright Tony Harrison (first published in the United States in 1988). Harrison relocates the action of *Lysistrata* to Greenham Common, the military airbase in Berkshire, Southern England, where a Women's Peace Camp was established in 1981 to protest against the deployment there of American cruise missiles. Raw in its emotions and forthright in its expression, *The Common Chorus* was never performed at its time of writing: production delays intervened and, as its author relates, 'the tension of a topical present . . . leached away into oblivion . . . [T]he Cold War . . . ended and my play [was] marooned in its moment'.[61] Lysistrata's complaints to the 'Inspector', too, so topical at the time with their references to 1980s unemployment and British 'yob culture', will also strike a modern reader as somewhat dated, even if the pacificist message still comes across loud and clear.[62]

> With Cruise missile money you could create jobs
> for kids your kind will end up calling 'yobs'.
> Their lives of unemployment don't make any sense
> and the money needed is squandered on 'Defence'.
> And by jobs I mean some profession other
> than killing the sons of a Spartan mother.

In fact, this was not Harrison's first attempt to pen an anti-war *Lysistrata*. *Aikin Mata*, his first version of the play (co-authored with the Irish poet James Simmons), was written while Harrison was working at Ahmadu Bello University in Northern Nigeria and performed in 1966 at a time of growing national tensions in the country.[63]

A twenty-first century adaption of the play, *Lisa's Sex Strike* by Blake Morrison, which premiered in Bolton, England in 2007, also wore its anti-war message on its sleeve. The fighting between whites and non-whites in Blackhurst, the fictional Northern English mill-town in which the play is set, is successfully quelled by Lisa (forcefully played in the original production by Becky Hindley). In *Lisa's Sex Strike*, the new enemy against which both sides unite is the local industrialist, Prutt (a figure inspired by Aristophanes' Prytanis), whose factory turns out to be secretly manufacturing weapons components for use in the Iraq War. In addition to an anti-Iraq War agenda, this adaptation contained a clear anti-establishment undercurrent, with extended mockery of the supposed incompetence of the British police.

(g) Lysistrata against the Iraq War: The Lysistrata Project (2003) and its afterlife

Topping any single translation, staging or reworking of the play in terms of its scale and scope is the Lysistrata Project, which played out in 2003. The brainchild of two US actors, Kathryn Blume and Sharron Bower, the initiative harnessed the new-found power of the internet to perform what they described as 'a theatrical act of dissent' in protest at the imminent invasion of Iraq by American-led allied forces.[64] As recorded on the Lysistrata Project website, their appeal to women around the world to '[d]o a reading of *Lysistrata* on March 3' was taken up in fifty-nine countries, involving some 300,000 participants worldwide, with events ranging from high-profile readings in New York and Athens to clandestine events in counties like China and Iraq itself.[65] In New York, for example, Blume and Bower took part in a reading at the Brooklyn Academy of Music's Harvey Theater, a carnival-like event which benefited from the participation of famous actors like Kevin Bacon and Kyra Sedgwick. The adaptation of the play used was that of Ellen McLaughlin, who 'condensed [*Lysistrata*] in order for it to be as quick-moving and as funny as possible'.[66] In Athens, a reading took place on the Pnyx, a venue which, as Lorna Hardwick notes, 'proclaimed the confidence of modern women in occupying and using a public space that in ancient Athens was the territory of men'.[67] In London a group of actors stood opposite the Houses of Parliament wearing gags, which they tore off before reading a section of the play (see Figure 5.4). In Columbus, Ohio, a father and his home-schooled son created *Lysisaurus*, a version of the play they staged in their basement using plastic dinosaurs.[68]

For a project that ostensibly began as a protest against the Iraq War, it is noteworthy that the agenda of the creators of the Lysistrata Project – as projected by their website at least – was avowedly feminist, as well as pacifist, with these feminist and pacifist agendas once more closely aligned. What is also strongly evident is the organizers' powerful belief in the need to take *action* if peace and women's rights are to be secured.

Figure 5.4 Gagged protestors assembled outside the Houses of Parliament in London, UK, on 3 March 2003 as part of the Lysistrata Project.

Indeed, seen in this light, the readings of *Lysistrata* might be viewed as a form of active protest in and of themselves – as well as a catalyst for further action.

One intriguing piece of afterlife that the Lysistrata Project enjoyed was a project organized by the Greek academic and dramaturg, Marina Kotzamani. In 2004, inspired by the readings of *Lysistrata* that she learnt had taken place in the Arab world as part of the project, she invited theatre practitioners, playwrights and theorists from across the Arab Mediterranean to write about how they would stage *Lysistrata* in their own countries. While the results, which were shared in a 2005 conference in Morocco, show a rich range of perspectives, certain themes emerged, such as globalization, US imperialism and the inadequacy of the model of war offered by Aristophanes to capture the complexity of modern conflicts.[69] What is striking once more is the way in which some participants integrated the play's themes of gender-conflict and peace in their treatments of the play. Ghada Amer, an Egyptian visual artist based in New York, and Riad Masarwi, a Palestinian playwright and director, both saw men as fuelling war through their natural, masculine aggression – a situation perpetuated by the patriarchal structures of contemporary society. In contrast, they credited women with a genuine desire for peace.[70] Another contributor to the project, the Egyptian playwright and film director, Lenin El-Ramly, was inspired to write a full play, *Salam El-Nisaa* ('A Peace of Women'), which was staged in Cairo in December 2004.[71] In El-Ramly's version, the women's gender ultimately causes their plan to fail since, as Kotzamani summarizes, 'decisions about war and peace rest with the powerful . . . who closely monitor the women's movements overtly, through brutal oppression, or covertly, through propaganda and spying.'[72] The gender politics of El-Ramly's play did not come through successfully for some critics, however, owing to the decision to cast men in some of the female roles.

(h) Making headlines in the twenty-first century: *Lysistrata* in the press, at the opera, on Broadway and on the big screen

Lysistrata is that rare example of an Aristophanic play known beyond academia, something it owes not only to the relative popularity it has enjoyed in the theatre – and its prominence in school and university syllabuses – but also to its memorable central conceit: put simply, *Lysistrata* is the play about the sex strike.[73] The play's fame in this reductive formula has led to another intriguing form of reception, as studied by Helen Morales: namely the evocation of *Lysistrata* in press coverage of contemporary attempts by women to use abstention from sex as a means to effect social and political change. Morales cites a number of examples of such campaigns, but her particular focus is on the reporting of the 'sex strike' that took place during Liberia's civil war in 2002, led by Leymah Gbowee, who went on to be awarded the Nobel Peace Prize in 2011 for her sustained efforts in furthering peace and women's rights in the country. In the press reports cited by Morales, Gbowee is described as 'a modern day Lysistrata'[74] and someone who 'persuaded many Liberian women to withhold sex from their warring menfolk unless they came to the negotiating table, a devastatingly successful campaign inspired by … Aristophanes' *Lysistrata*'.[75] In fact, Gbowee later claimed to have been unaware of *Lysistrata* at the time of the 'sex strike', her first contact with the play being a copy bought for her as a gift some years later.[76] In making comparisons between the Liberian situation and *Lysistrata*, however, journalists set two distinct (if complementary) processes in play. First, and most obviously, they invite their readers to view modern events through an ancient lens. But importantly, too, these press reports tacitly signal how *Lysistrata* – the ancient lens itself – is to be understood: namely as a play which is reducible to the formula of an 'anti-war sex strike' and one which can be comfortably aligned with modern causes such as twenty-first-century feminism and contemporary campaigns for peace.[77]

As well as professional and amateur stagings of the play, the early twenty-first century saw a variety of adaptations of *Lysistrata* that went beyond conventional theatre, radically reconfiguring the plot of the play in intriguing ways. These include a comic opera, *Lysistrata, or The Nude Goddess* by Mark Adamo (staged at Houston Grand Opera and New York City Opera in 2005 and 2006 respectively), in which the central character, Lysia, devises the sex strike largely to exact revenge on her lover, the Athenian general, Nico.[78] Critics generally praised the ambition of the piece, though reactions were more mixed to its rhyme-filled, clever dialogue, its bawdy comedy and its (largely energetic) score. Based only loosely on Aristophanes' play, the opera ends with Nico and his lieutenant, Kinesias, killing one another during the drunken festivities – only to be resurrected by Ares and Aphrodite. These gods then deliver a message to mortals which is at best bittersweet: peace is fleeting, so enjoy it while it lasts ('Never will it end, never, never; time to time there may be peace, but there never will be peace'). Also notable for its distinctive take on the play is the much-hyped musical *Lysistrata Jones*, which officially opened on Broadway in December 2011 only to close in January 2012. The action of this piece of theatre played out in the fictional Athens university, where the cheerleader Lysistrata Jones, or Lyssie J, leads a sex strike to incentivize the men's basketball team to end their losing streak of thirty years. If these twenty-first-century retellings of *Lysistrata* seem less than politically charged, however, then the first feature film ever to be produced by Amazon Studios was about to prove that *Lysistrata* could still be adapted to deliver a hard-hitting message in the twenty-first century. Released in 2015, the movie in question was *Chi-raq* (see Figure 5.5).

Chi-raq sees *Lysistrata* reconceived by director Spike Lee as a disturbing, emotionally charged and sassy movie, exploring the devastating effect of black-on-black gun crime on a community in Chicago. The word Chi-raq, which combines the elements 'Chicago' and 'Iraq', was already in existence before Lee's film; its significance is explored in the opening credits, which inform the viewer that while 2,349 Americans died in the Afghanistan war between 2001 and 2015 and 4,424 in the Iraq war from 2003 to 2011, 7,356 people were murdered in Chicago in a similar period (2001–15). In the film, Chi-raq is also the stage name of a rapper (Demetrius Dupree played by Nick Cannon). He is the boyfriend of Lysistrata (played by Teyonah Parris in a much-acclaimed performance) who has a political awakening following the accidental shooting of a young girl by two rival gangs: the Spartans, led by Chi-raq, and the Trojans, led by a character called Cyclops (an eyepatch-wearing Wesley Snipes).

Chi-raq is hard-hitting, combining a hip-hop soundtrack, gun violence and prolonged scenes of high emotion, such as an eight-minute-long anti-gun sermon delivered by the preacher at Patti's funeral.[79] There is palpable sexual tension between Lysistrata and Chi-raq, too, with large crowd scenes, offbeat comedy and pointed moments of escapist fantasy thrown into the mix (such as when Lysistrata pretends to seduce an ageing white supremacist, named General King Kong, and ends up tying him, blindfolded, to the barrel of a cannon, stripped down to a pair of confederate flag boxer shorts).[80] For Helen Morales *Chi-raq* is 'a shocking, stylized morality tale' with 'a chaotic energy that can be overwhelming but ensures sustained passion, vitality and tension';[81] for Alyssa Rosenburg, 'a patently bonkers movie' whose 'power lies in its stylistic lunacy and political defiance'.[82] Certainly it succeeded in stoking controversy – not least in Chicago for the way it portrays the city.[83]

Classical allusions – not always borrowed faithfully from Aristophanes' play – are scattered throughout the film, with Samuel L. Jackson providing additional 'Greek' framing as a dapperly dressed narrator called Dolmedes. In a programmatic piece to camera at the beginning of the movie, he declares:

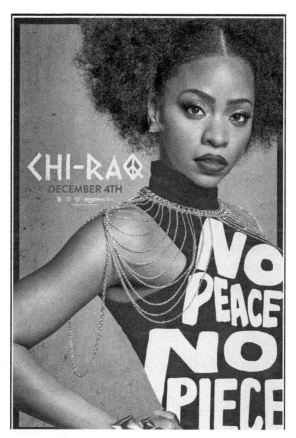

Figure 5.5 Film poster of *Chi-raq* (2015) directed by Spike Lee, featuring Teyonah Parris as Lysistrata.

In the year 411 BC
(That's before baby Jesus, y'all),
The Greek Aristophanes penned a play
Satirizing his day,
And in the style of his time,
'Stophanes made that shit rhyme.
Transplanted today we retain his verse,
To show our love for the universe.

Rhyme (though not a feature of Aristophanes' own verse, of course) is indeed used as a leitmotif throughout the film, which also boasts some memorable slogans summing up the women's demands: 'No peace, no piece!' (which appeared on posters advertising the film: see Figure 5.5) and 'No peace, no pussy!' (which did not). Interestingly, too, the women's seizure of the city's armoury (mirroring their ancient counterparts' capture of the Acropolis) sparks a global movement conveyed in the film by footage reminiscent of the media coverage of the Lysistrata Project (which, of course, was connected to Iraq rather than Chi-raq). Part of Lysistrata's social awakening, too, is prompted by her discovery online of another example of non-violent protest by women, the Liberian sex strike, led by Leymah Gbowee. *Chi-raq* might thus be said to pay homage not just to Aristophanes' *Lysistrata* itself, but also to the reception tradition it created.

(i) Conclusion: *Lysistrata*'s long-term allure

This chapter has aimed to paint a picture, in broad brush strokes, of the reception history of *Lysistrata* in the English-speaking world and beyond over the course of nearly 200 years. Specialist studies in this area abound: work which examines the reception of *Lysistrata* in the United States and Greece, for example,[84] or traces the tradition of cinematic or musical adaptations of *Lysistrata*,[85] or explores particular adaptations, productions of the play or cultural phenomena such as the Lysistrata Project.[86] Individual studies and general overviews usefully feed off one another: both identify themes and points of interest which can then underpin further, informed analysis of the welter of receptions that *Lysistrata* has generated.

One of the key themes to emerge in this chapter is the different ways in which Lysistrata (and the other women in the play) are reconfigured either to fit with or, alternatively, challenge prevailing gender norms in particular historic and cultural contexts. *Lysistrata's* women have been presented as sexy and alluring (in titillating revue shows in Paris and Athens), as good wives who provide stability for their communities (in *The Second Greatest Sex*, for example), as powerful change-makers who challenge authority (in feminist-leaning and protest-driven versions), as wives and mothers affected by war (in pacificist-leaning stagings) and, importantly, as *combinations* of some or all of these things. The play has thus repeatedly served as a platform for exploring, modelling or challenging what it is, or might be, to be a woman at a given point of time in a given society, sometimes providing comfortable conclusions (for some audience members at least), at other times posing questions that are awkward or unanswerable. With all its gender inequality and heteronormativity, the model of domestic life to which the central characters in *The Second Greatest Sex* return once the fighting is done is presented as cosy and appealing, for example, whereas the fractured conclusion of Spiderwoman's *Lysistrata Numbah!* self-consciously challenges the possibility of a one-size-fits-all happy ending. As Muriel Miguel, one of the cast members, explains:[87]

> So the show's ending, it went like, 'OK, the war is over, you can go back to your man, and you can go back to your man.' But the people go, 'Mmm, uh, wait a minute Lisa-strata, suppose we don't want to go back.' And someone goes, 'Suppose I want to go home with *her*?' Someone else says, 'Suppose I don't want to go home *at all*?' Lisa-strata says, 'This is disgusting! This is what we fought for!' But someone says, 'This is what *you* fought for.'

A key benefit that studying the reception of *Lysistrata* provides is that questions raised by later adaptations of the play can be asked of the original text, too, often providing us with fresh perspectives on Aristophanes' work. Aristophanes' women arguably display all the attributes listed above, for example – they are sexy and alluring, good wives who provide social stability, change-makers *and* victims of war – but how did Aristophanes present and tailor these female qualities for his own audience? To what extent do his characters conform to or subvert his own culture's attitudes towards women? How cosy or awkward might the original audience of *Lysistrata* have found the play's ending?

The discussion in this chapter has amply revealed the incredible popularity of *Lysistrata* over the last 100 or so years. The play's distinctive plotline – as well as its unusual status as classical-yet-risqué – have no doubt underpinned this appeal, as has the fact that *Lysistrata* largely 'works' for a modern audience in terms of its structure and characterization (in a way that is not true for all Aristophanic comedies: see Chapter 1 Section A). A further important factor, as we have repeatedly seen, is that *Lysistrata* allows feminist and pacificist perspectives to be explored, providing writers, directors, readers and audiences with an ancient example – albeit a fictional and fantastical one – of what women might do and say if they hold power and how resistance to war might be expressed. Bringing these two threads together, the play can also been viewed as providing an ancient precedent – albeit, once again, fictional and fantastical – for female-led, mass protest (as its associations with the suffragist movement, the Greenham Common protests and Lysistrata Project indicate). The play has also provided a platform, borrowed from what is often perceived as the 'high-brow' culture of classical Greece, for the discussion of sex, allowing writers and audiences to toy with themes and ideas that in their own cultures are illicit or taboo.

What does the future hold in store for *Lysistrata*? While aspects of the play will no doubt continue to appeal, *Lysistrata* also has qualities which may well make it problematic for twenty-first-century audiences. The Battle of the Sexes theme, for example, sits somewhat uneasily in a world where gender is increasingly seen as a spectrum (or something more nuanced still) rather than a binary construct. As the roles of men, women and other genders continue to shift, how well will the traditional stereotypes in the play work for future audiences: the equation of women with the home and men with political power, for example? Crucially, too, while the stereotypical portrayal of women in *Lysistrata* has regularly been seen as problematic, what is seldom highlighted is the unflattering way in which men are characterized in the play: they are portrayed as warmongers and bullies, mocked for their insensitivity and ineffectiveness, and ultimately become ruled and blinded by their sexual urges. This is hardly a nuanced portrayal of masculinity and one wonders how acceptable future audiences will find it – as well as the fact that the male sex is set up so squarely in the play as a target for full-blooded abuse. Looking beyond gender issues in the play, there is also the way in which war is characterized: as was highlighted above (Section G), the model of war presented in *Lysistrata* arguably fails to capture the nature or complexity of many modern conflicts. Will the Peloponnesian War that forms the backdrop to the play continue to have resonance for those caught up in, or looking to oppose, future conflicts? Only time will tell, but in case we are ever tempted to write *Lysistrata* off, we would do well to recall the vast range of ways in which it has already spoken to writers, directors and audiences over the years and just how seductive a play it has repeatedly proven to be.

Notes

Chapter 1

1   The scholarly consensus is that five comedies were staged each year at the Lenaea and five at the City Dionysia, with this number *perhaps* reduced to three at each festival at various points during the Peloponnesian War (a point which remains controversial: see Csapo and Slater 1998: 107 and Hartwig 2019: 215). The competition was decided by the votes of ten judges, one appointed by lot from each of Athens' ten tribes, with prizes awarded to the playwright and sponsor of the victorious play. Our knowledge of the voting system is sketchy, but it seems that a small number of votes – perhaps five – were initially chosen at random in an attempt to determine a winner. Interestingly, in ancient victory lists it is the names of the winning play along with its *chorēgos* (sponsor/producer) and *didaskalos* (director) that are recorded; therefore the playwright's name only appeared if he had produced the play himself (a task which tragic poets seemed to embrace more readily than comic playwrights). For a broad overview of the comic competition, see Robson 2009: 13–29.

2   The system of liturgy in Athens relied on wealthy individuals to provide a public service (*leitourgia*) by financing an element of civic or military life, such as the equipping of a trireme or the sponsorship of tragic or comic plays. Unlike the Dionysia, metics (resident immigrants) as well as citizens could act as a *chorēgos*, 'sponsor' (lit. 'chorus leader') at the Lenaea. On the role of the *chorēgos*, see Wilson 2000, esp. 50–103.

3   See Halliwell 1980.

4   It is also possible that Aristophanes won first prize with *Babylonians* at the Lenaea in 426 BCE; see Storey 2019: 16.

5   The Greek terms are *archaia*, *mesē* and *nea kōmōidia* (cf. Aristotle *Ethics* 1128a22–5, where comedy is simply divided into *palaia*, 'ancient', and *kainē*, 'modern'). Aristophanes' fourth-century BCE plays, *Assemblywomen* and *Wealth*, are sometimes classed by scholars as Middle Comedy.

6   E.g. *Wasps* 65–6, *Clouds* 522 and 547–8; *Clouds* 553–9.

7   A phrase coined by Arrowsmith 1973: 137.

8   There also seems to have been a split chorus in Eupolis' *Maricas* (staged in
    421 BCE). The chorus of Aristophanes' *Acharnians* also temporarily divides
    into two competing factions at lines 557–77 (though as Olson 2002 ad loc.
    points out, the division in opinion may simply have been staged as a
    confrontation between two individual chorus members).

9   It is only the other 'women' plays that are less well preserved:
    Assemblywomen survives in seven manuscripts and *Thesmophoriazusae*
    only in the Ravenna manuscript (which contains all eleven surviving plays)
    and a late copy of it. Three small fragments of ancient texts of *Lysistrata* also
    survive: see Henderson 1980: l–li. Interest in the play in the ancient world
    seems to have been limited, too. Beyond the scholia on the play, the
    scattered references to *Lysistrata* are largely confined to the works of
    grammarians and lexicographers.

10 See e.g. Olson 2012: 73–4. Revermann 2006: 70 and 258–9 suggests that the
    text of the play that has come down to us might be a version of the play
    performed in the fourth century BCE, perhaps in the Spartan colony of
    Taras in Southern Italy. See chapter 2 section J.

11 On *Lysistrata*'s songs, see Parker 1997.

12 See Dover 1972: 6–12 and Revermann 2006: 320–5.

13 See Revermann 2006: 254–60 who summarizes the scholarly debate and
    discusses the difficulties posed by the ending of the play.

14 See esp. lines 497–501. The verb *sōizō* is also used at lines 41 and 525 of
    the play, *sōteria*, 'salvation', 'safety' at line 30 and *sōs*, 'safe', at 488 (taken
    together, these words cover the idea of 'saving' in a range of senses: political,
    military, personal and religious). Instructively, the speech attributed to
    Peisander at Thucydides 8.53, delivered at the Assembly not long after
    Lysistrata was performed, twice invokes the notion of Athens' 'salvation'
    (*sōteria*).

15 Marathon formed part of the Tetrapolis (Four Towns), an ancient
    confederacy of neighbouring communities in eastern Attica; see
    Sommerstein 1990: note on line 285 ad loc.

16 A notable omission from the major conflicts of the Persian Wars mentioned
    in *Lysistrata* is the Battle of Plataea in which, as Sommerstein 1977: 121
    comments, the Boeotians (who are envisaged in *Lysistrata* as one of the
    city-states that will contribute to the Pan-Hellenic truce) 'were rather too
    prominent on the wrong [i.e. Persian] side'.

17 See Sommerstein 1990: note on lines 678 and 679 ad loc. and Bowie 1993:
    184.

18 It was a bad smell inflicted on the women by Aphrodite that led the men of Lemnos to abandon their wives for enslaved women from Thrace; an event which in turn led the wholesale massacre of all the men on the island apart from King Thoas, who was secretly saved by his daughter, Hypsipyle. See further Bowie 1993: 186–201 on the various ways that this myth is evoked in *Lysistrata*.

19 Referring to the fortunes of Athenians who struggled financially during the Peloponnesian War, the speaker of Demosthenes 57.45 says that 'many women became nurses, wool-workers and grape-pickers because of the city's misfortunes in those times, including citizen women (*astai gunaikes*)'.

20 See Henderson 1987b: 108–9, 117 and 120–1.

21 For an overview of prostitution in classical Athens, see Robson 2013: 67–89.

22 For discussion, see Sommerstein 1977 and Austin and Olson 2004: xxxiii–lxiv.

23 On Athens' Lenaea festival and the question of where its dramatic competitions were staged, see le Guen 2019. One notable difference between the dramatic competitions at this festival and those held at the Dionysia was that metics (resident immigrants) could serve as both chorus members and *chorēgoi* (see note 2 above). The fact that the Lenaea took place well before the beginning of the sailing season makes it plausible the theatre audiences would have been smaller and more local in character than those at the Dionysia.

24 See Marshall 2014: 136 on the possibility that Lenaea plays were staged at the Sanctuary of Dionysus Lenaios. Habash 2019 provides a brief overview of the evidence and scholarly debate.

25 Estimates include 3,700 (Dawson 1997: 7), 5,500 (Korres 2002: 540) and 4,000–7,000 (Csapo in Csapo and Goette 2007: 97). The capacity of the fourth-century BCE stone theatre is generally estimated to be 14,000–17,000.

26 The scattered references in ancient sources to the so-called 'view from the poplar', a space on the slopes of the Acropolis beyond the bleachers (i.e., wooden seats of the theatre) from which spectators could watch for free (or low cost), are discussed by Scullion 1994: 56–7 and Roselli 2011: 72–5. Roselli's estimate is that a crowd of perhaps 2,000 or so might have watched the plays in this way. See also Robson 2017: 70–1.

27 *Frogs* 676–7; the figure of 13,000 which appears at Aristophanes' *Wealth* 1082 may also represent an estimate of the total size of the audience.

28 Sommerstein 1997 and 2017, esp. 14–22.

29 Thus Henderson 2019. For discussions of this perennially hot potato, see
    e.g. Henderson 1991b, Goldhill 1994, Carter 2011: 50–3, and Roselli 2011:
    158–94. As Sommerstein 1997: 65 states: 'whether or not their audience
    actually was male or even nearly so, dramatists seem to regard it as such . . .
    dramatists, tragic and comic alike, wrote as male Athenian citizens for male
    Athenian citizens'; see also Sommerstein 2017, 13–14.

30 For a concise overview of the controversies surrounding the shape of the
    orchēstra, the number of doors and presence or absence of a stage, see
    Marshall 2014: 135–6. Certainly, a single set of double doors is sufficient for
    staging *Lysistrata*.

31 Textual references such as *Knights* 147–9 (where a character is invited
    to come 'up') are also used to support the notion of a fifth-century
    stage.

32 Wiles 1997: 63–86 and 2000: 106; Storey and Allan 2005: 37–8.

33 Henderson 1980: 160 lists a number of sequences in the play which appear
    to contain four or five speaking roles. Dover 1972: 155–6 highlights two
    passages in the play which he suggests either require five speaking actors or
    some doubling up if only four are used: lines 430–49 and 728–61.
    MacDowell 1994, however, argues that all scenes in surviving comedy (with
    few, if any, exceptions) can be performed by four speaking actors, including
    the relevant scenes in *Lysistrata* (331–3).

34 Taplin 1978: 3.

35 These various objects take centre stage at lines 199–239 (the cup); 327–86
    (the pitchers); and 916–49 (the Myrrhine's bedroom accoutrements).

36 Wiles 2000: 149.

Chapter 2

1   Rouge ('alkanet') is mentioned at line 48, but white lead was also used by
    women in the classical era to make skin look paler. At lines 827–8 the leader
    of the chorus of old women mentions a different method
    of female depilation when she boasts that her 'man-bag' is not hairy,
    but rather 'singed clean with the lamp'. For a summary of the scholarly
    debates surrounding female depilation in the classical era, see Robson
    2013: 121–2.

2   Stroup 2004; McClure 2015: 66.

3   This memorable phrase may well be an Aristophanic coinage, designed to
     raise both a laugh and an eyebrow. Arguing persuasively against the
     established view that the image conjured up is of a woman bending forward
     with her rear raised, reminiscent of a lion ready to pounce (e.g. Henderson
     1987a and Sommerstein 1990: note on lines 231–2 ad loc.), Prince 2009
     suggests that a 'lioness' is better understood as a woman in control of the
     sexual act, astride the man, with the '(cheese-)grating' equating to pleasure-
     giving grinding – which, of course, the women's husbands are to be denied.

4   On women and sacrifice in *Lysistrata*, see Fletcher 1999, esp. 112–14 and
     115–17. See also Figure 1.4, which depicts a scene from Aristophanes'
     Thesmophoriazusae (staged the same year as *Lysistrata*) and also combines
     the theme of sacrifice with women's supposed love
     of alcohol. At line 753 of the play, a wineskin dressed like a baby is sacrificed
     in imitation of a similar scene in Euripides' lost tragedy, *Telephus*.

5   This sudden shift in location is not at all uncommon in comedy, especially
     in the prologues of plays which are 'a place where space is
     still in the process of being created' (Lowe 2006: 52).

6   Prior to line 204, the setting might be thought of as the street outside
     Lysistrata's or Calonice's house, or alternatively as an anonymous or 'atopic'
     location (Lowe 2006: 52) – until, that is, a verbal cue gives the stage doors a
     specific identity in a moment of 'refocusing' (Dale 1956).

7   The fleet was Athens' 'wooden wall' – at least on one interpretation of the
     oracle given to the Athenians by the Priestess of Apollo at Delphi on the eve
     of Xerxes' attempted invasion of the Greek mainland. This prophecy also
     strongly hinted that 'Holy Salamis' would be the site
     of a significant sea battle. On the back of this, Themistocles encouraged the
     Athenians to invest in Athens' fleet: Herodotus 7.141–4.

8   Faraone 1997.

9   See Chapter 1 note 14.

10   Intriguingly, one of the Probouloi happened to be the tragic poet Sophocles.

11   That Peisander is mentioned in a casual put down at line 490 is generally
     taken as evidence that Aristophanes did not know of the general's
     revolutionary plans when this line was written: see Chapter 2 Section B.

12   In classical Athens, first-time brides were generally teenagers, with 14–16
     perhaps being a typical age for a girl to be married. A first-time groom was
     more typically in his late twenties to mid-thirties. See Robson 2013: 16.

13   As Sommerstein 2009b: 238–40 asserts, '[t]he prolonged nudity of a whole
     semi-chorus is quite unlike anything else in the corpus', adding that by

undressing the men are supposedly looking to 'assert their masculinity'; what they reveal, however, are old and feeble bodies. The women are not to be outdone and arguably 'assert … their equality' by following the men's lead.

14   The animals with which women are equated include: a flounder (115), an eel (702), swallows (771), a leopard (1015) and foals (1307) – not forgetting a lioness (on a cheesegrater) (231–2). On animal imagery in the play, see Gilhuly 2009 170–6.

15   Vaio 1973: 376

16   Thus Tsoumpra 2020: 12–13. Bowie 1993: 199 concurs, but sees additional symbolism in the helmet, arguing that it underlines contradictions in the various roles of women in the play (e.g. as mothers, warriors, and so on).

17   The historian Herodotus (8.41.2–3) relates how, at the time of the Persian invasion in 480 BCE, the honey-cake traditionally offered to the serpent remained unconsumed, which the Athenians took as a sign that Athena had fled the city and, consequently, that they should evacuate the city themselves.

18   It was in the ancient Temple of Athena Polias (the western end of which seems to have survived the fire of 480 BCE and was subsequently patched up) that the fabled guardian serpent was once said to have lived: Herodotus 8.41.2.

19   On oracles in Aristophanes, see Muecke 1998 and Eidinow 2019.

20   Hawkins 2002 discusses the names used in these odes. Since Melanion was one of the names by which the successful suitor of the mythical Atalanta was known, he suggests that Aristophanes is deliberately undermining the old men's claim that he is a misogynist, laying them open to attack. And since Timon was the name of a renowned misanthrope rather than hater of men per se, Hawkins argues that the woman's ode shows them to be cleverly manipulating language in order to appropriate him as a kindred spirit, i.e. by presenting him as a social outsider hostile to *men* in particular rather than *mankind* in general.

21   For *murtia* as a slang term for female genitalia, see Henderson 1991a: 134–5.

22   Indeed, this Myrrhine seems to have been the first ever Priestess of Athena Nike (whose temple is on the Acropolis), appointed at some point in the 420s BCE (whether this post was annually renewed or a longer-term appointment, making Myrrhine a recent or even the incumbent role-holder

is unclear). Sommerstein 1990: 5 n. 31 and Henderson 1987a: xl–xli are both dubious that audience members would have made a connection between the historical figure and Aristophanic character; Smith 2017: 38–9 and Thonemann 2020: 133–4 take the opposite view, however.

23 Stroup 2004: 56–62; Faraone 2006: 210 and 216 and Gilhuly 2009: 159–61.

24 Silk calls these kind of comic lyrics 'hybrids' (2000: 180) or 'low lyrics *plus*' (1980: 133).

25 Tsoumpra 2020: 3–13 suggests that the effects of the women's abstention from sex in *Lysistrata* are also presented as an illness which only intercourse will ultimately cure. She highlights the use of medicalized language in connection with the women, too, such as *binētiōmen* (715), 'we need a fuck', a comic formation based on contemporary verbs ending in -*iaō* also designating maladies.

26 On this passage as a sexual assault fantasy, see Robson 2015: 322–3. *Psōle* signifies a penis which is erect inasmuch as it has a retracted foreskin.

27 For discussion, see Henderson 1980: 184–5 and Sommerstein 1990: note on lines 982ff. ad loc.

28 Or possibly 'walking stick' (Sommerstein 1990 on line 991 ad loc.). As has been noted by Tsoumpra (2020: 14–15), this scene turns an Old Comic convention on its head. More commonly in Aristophanes an erect phallus acts as a symbol of an old man's rejuvenated libido; In *Lysistrata*, however, young men try to hide their erections under clothes or explain them away.

29 Sommerstein 1990: note on line 996 ad loc. detects a possible pun on *estukanti*, 'have erections', and *hestakanti*, 'are standing idle, failing to act'.

30 Sommerstein 1990: 5.

31 The gnat is described as coming from Tricorythus, a deme adjacent to Marathon.

32 Sommerstein 2009b: 245 and 2010: 47. Hall 2010: 34 remarks that, 'by the end of the play [Lysistrata's] persona seems to merge . . . with the actual goddess herself'. Faraone 2006: 218, who points out that the primary meaning of *iunx* is an 'erotic magic spell', suggests that Lysistrata is being envisaged, in part, as an 'autonomous courtesan, using a iunx to lead her boyfriends unerringly to herself'.

33 Once again, scholars have observed that Lysistrata is cast in a pimp role here, e.g. Faraone 2006: 219 who refers to her as a 'madam extraordinaire' and the Acropolis as her 'brothel'.

34 For discussion of these figures and how they might have been represented on stage see, for example, Zweig 1992: 78–81 and Revermann 2006: 157–9.

35 Lysistrata talks of 'enemies at hand with their barbarian hosts' (1133), which Sommerstein 1990: note on line 1133 ad loc. suggests is probably a reference to the two Persian satraps Tissaphernes and Pharnabazus, and their attempts following the Sicilian disaster to dislodge Greek cities in Asia Minor from the Athenian Empire (see Chapter 2 Section B). Tellingly, there is no specific allusion to Peisander's and Alcibiades' covert negotiations with Persia about which Aristophanes, along with most other Athenians, was most likely ignorant at the time of production.

36 Henderson 1987a: note on lines 1133–4 ad loc.

37 The earthquake took place in 464 BCE and Cimon's intervention probably in early 462 BCE.

38 As Sommerstein 2009a: 228–9 notes, the deal is hardly even-handed. Whereas the Spartans simply seek the return of Pylos, which was captured by Athens in 425 BCE, the Athenians seek to gain two territories which had never been under their control (Echinos and the Malian Gulf) and a third (the Walls of Megara) which they had only ever held for brief periods in the past.

39 On the (much discussed) power dynamics in this passage, see e.g. Zweig 1992: 80–1; Stroup 2004: 62–8; and Lambert 2018.

40 Dover 1972: 154.

41 Vaio 1973: 378.

42 For discussion, see Russo 1994: 184–5 and Henderson 1980: 216.

43 E.g. Wilamowitz 1927 and Henderson 1980 who, in their respective commentaries, give these lines to a Prytanis. While Russo 1994: 169–73 notes that in the Ravenna and Parisian manuscripts the siglum of Lysistrata stands before these lines, he is also of the view that a male character speaks them (an Athenian Ambassador) and, what is more, that Lysistrata is absent from this scene. Halliwell 1997: 140 similarly gives these lines (without comment) to an 'Athenian'. Sommerstein 2009b: 244 offers a spirited defence of his decision, suggesting that 'it would be extraordinary if . . . Lysistrata were suddenly, in the final scene, to be kept silent'.

44 Lysistrata's mention of a 'husband' (*anēr*) at 514 is arguably generic (since she is talking about the experiences of women as a whole), but might equally be taken to imply that she herself is married. Later, the men whose 'talk' she claims to have learnt much from include her father and older men (1126), with no specific mention of a husband. See also Chapter 3 note 11.

45 E.g. Henderson 1987a: note on line 1321 ad loc. and Sommerstein 1990: note on lines 1320–1 ad loc.

46   Revermann 2006: 258.

47   Arguably, a final hymn to the goddess makes for an equally fitting
     conclusion regardless of whether Lysistrata did or did not lend an
     Athena-like presence to this scene.

Chapter 3

1   Hall 2010: 29; Henderson 1987a: xxxvii–xxxviii.

2   On various mythical and historical female figures drawn on by
    Aristophanes in his creation of Lysistrata, see Hall 2010.

3   On the theme of sacrifice in the play, see Fletcher 1999.

4   Lewis 1955.

5   Sommerstein's 2009a: 235 preferred translations are 'she who resolves strife'
    and 'she who scatters armies', though these obviously capture less well in
    English the similar form that the names share in Greek.

6   The name also appears at Aristophanes, *Peace* 992; Smith 2017: 36 n.9
    suggests that both in *Peace* and *Lysistrata*, Lysismache is better understood
    as an (otherwise unattested) epithet of the goddess Peace rather a reference
    to the real-life Priestess.

7   Henderson 1987: xxxix.

8   Thus Sommerstein 2009b: 243–4.

9   E.g. Sommerstein 2009b: 245–6 and Hall 2010: 35. A celebrated incident
    involving the Priestess of Athena Polias occurred in 508 BCE, when King
    Cleomenes of Sparta had retreated to the Acropolis having failed in his
    attempt to intervene in the affairs of Athens' fledgling democracy.
    Herodotus tells us that when Cleomenes tried to enter the temple of Athena
    Polias, the Priestess rose from her chair, crying 'Spartan stranger, go back:
    do not enter the holy place! It is not lawful for Dorians to enter here.' (5.72).
    Cleomenes departed Athens two days later: see Chapter 1 Section C and
    Chapter 2 Section I.

10 Sommerstein 1990: note on line 7 ad loc. Henderson 1980: 166 on the other
    hand suggests the term simply signifies 'friend'. The original audience would
    have been much better placed than modern scholars to judge which age
    bracket Lysistrata fell into, of course, since her hair colour and hairstyle
    would have given a clear indication of her stage of life (e.g. young and
    unmarried, a more mature married woman or a grey-haired older woman).

11 Scholars regularly distance themselves from the idea that Lysistrata is married. Smith 2017: 37, for instance, states that 'Lysistrata's marital status is never revealed in the play', though (unlike some) he does admit the possibility she might be a widow. It is true that Lysistrata is to an extent speaking generically in lines 507–20, describing the kind of conversations that wives used to have with their husbands, but she nevertheless says at least once that '*I* kept quiet' (i.e. not 'we': *kagō* in line 515; editors routinely supply *egō*, too, in 516 as the subject of the verb *esigōn* 'I/they kept quiet'). What is more, at line 519 she personalizes her narrative again by saying that the husband in question 'gave *me* (*m'*) an angry look'.) See also Chapter 2 note 44.

12 IG II² 3453 line 4. The words '[Lysimache] mother of ... from Phlya' (a deme in North-West Athens) appear in line 5. While Lysistrata does (generically) refer to mothers giving birth to sons who are sent out as soldiers (588–9), at lines 18–19, Calonice must remind her about the difficulties for a woman trying to leave the house when she has a baby.

13 Or as Sommerstein 1990: 5 puts it, the relationship between the real and fictional women is best characterized as one of 'association and reminiscence'. Rutherford 2015: 63 similarly argues for 'a looser and less direct or allegorical relationship between the character and the real Athenian priestess'.

14 For both Henderson 1987 and Sommerstein 1990, the attributions of these lines to Lysistrata are uncontroversial; Wilson 2007, however, gives the lines to Calonice (following a suggestion by MacDowell 1995: 230 n. 4 and supported by Thonemann 2020: 131 n. 20). The idea in these lines is probably that Lysistrata has not even seen a modest-sized dildo (i.e. one that is five inches in length – or 'eight fingers', i.e. finger breadths, as the Greek has it), let alone a decent-sized one.

15 Sommerstein 2009a and 2010.

16 Hall 2010: 36.

17 Thucydides 8.70–1 and 8.90–1. For a useful summary of these events, see Sommerstein 2009a: 230–1.

18 Spartan duplicity is alluded to both in other passages in Aristophanes, e.g. *Acharnians* 307–8 and *Peace* 623 and elsewhere, e.g. Euripides, *Andromache* 445–53.

19 The proposal to amend the text of the treaty was put forward by Alcibiades and provided justification for an (arguably unwise) intervention in a conflict between Epidauros (where Sparta had stationed a garrison, provoking the Athenian allegation of truce-breaking) and Argos (an ally of

Athens). This chain of events, including the Battle of Mantinea (418 BCE), only narrowly avoided sparking a full-scale resumption of hostilities between Athens and Sparta (see Chapter 2 Section B).

20   The importance of the tyrannicides to classical Athenians might be judged from the fact these bronze figures of Harmodius and Aristogeiton comprised 'the first two statues erected in Greece dedicated not to mythical figures, but to historical people' (Lear and Cantarella 2008: 15). When the original statues were taken back to Persia following the sack of Athens in 480 BCE, they were also considered important enough quickly to replace. Two variations of the drinking songs celebrating the tyrannicides have come down to us: PMG 893 and 895.

21   Xenophon, *Constitution of the Spartans* 1.4.

22   See also Henderson 1980: 165 as well as Plutarch, *Lycurgus* 14–15 (who claims that Spartan girls exercised and attended processions in the nude).

23   Herodotus 1.82.8; Xenophon, *Constitution of the Spartans* 11.3. Cleomenes is also described as 'hairy-faced' at line 279. The red cloak of Spartan soldiers is also mentioned at line 1140.

24   Lampito herself has a name that hints at nobility: Herodotus 6.71.2 tells us that this had also been the name of the mother of one of the current kings of Sparta, Agis II.

25   The study of Aristophanes' representation of non-Attic Greek is further complicated by the question of (a) whether Aristophanes originally wrote using the old Attic alphabet or the Ionic alphabet which eventually became standard in Athens, and (b) the extent to which later editors might have attempted to 'correct' or standardize the text. See Colvin 1999: 95–116, who takes the view that Aristophanes wrote in Ionic script and that the text is unlikely to have been subject to significant editorial alterations.

26   Colvin 1999: 297. See Harvey 1994: 44–6 and esp. Colvin 1999: 119–263 for analyses of the Laconian in *Lysistrata*.

27   In approximately seventy lines of spoken Laconian, the oath *nai tō siō*, 'by the two gods', appears no fewer than ten times.

28   Harvey 1994: 46.

29   Colvin 1999: 299–300 concludes that there is no attempt by Aristophanes to portray the speakers of other Greek dialects as speaking 'bad Greek', either, in contrast to the Greek spoken by barbarian characters, which might be misunderstood or misinterpreted for comic effect. Willi 2003: 139–41 suggests that Spartan dialect in speech (which is initially associated with the women's conspiracy in the play) would have had negative connotations for

an audience, but that its use in song towards the end of the play would have
had the opposite effect.

30 Harvey 1994: 51.

31 Rosen 2018: 146. He also suggests that the poets wish 'to alienate neither
pro-Spartan Athenians in the audience nor their committed opponents'
(Rosen 2018: 148).

32 See Chapter 2 note 38.

33 Sommerstein 1996.

34 See Sommerstein 1997 and 2017 and Robson 2017: 69–74.

35 For an overview of the issues thrown up by Aristophanic politics, see
Robson 2009: 162–87, and for a deft survey and critique of scholarship in
this area, see Olson 2010, esp. 46–59.

36 The main target here is *hetaireiai*, 'brotherhoods', also known as
sunōmosiai, i.e. 'sworn groups' of young, upper-class men who provided
each other with 'mutual aid in lawsuits (*dikē*) and in gaining political office
(*archē*)'. Peisander persuaded a number of these 'to rally together and
jointly resolve to overthrow the democracy' later in 411 BCE (Thucydides
8.54.4).

37 Sommerstein 1990: note on line 582 ad loc. and Henderson 1987a: 144 note
on lines 582–6 ad loc.

38 Dover 1972: 161 attempts to bring various threads in the play together by
suggesting that Lysistrata is implying in this speech that peace is best
negotiated from a position of strength, which an extension of the citizen
franchise would secure.

39 Olson 2010: 47 suggests that, while Aristophanes' plays have no 'practical
political agenda', they nevertheless represent 'raucous interventions in what
looks to be vigorous public debate about life in the city'.

40 Sommerstein 1977: 124.

41 Gilhuly's argument (2009: 149–53) also depends on the idea that Myrrhine
was seemingly the name of the first ever Priestess of Athena Nike (see
Chapter 2 Section G and Chapter 2 note 22). Importantly for her argument,
the holder of this post was determined by lot from all eligible Athenian
women (i.e. 'democratically') rather than by birth into a particular
aristocratic family.

42 Gilhuly 2009: 147. On the nature of these religious roles, see Sommerstein
1990: note on lines 642–6 ad loc.

43 Gilhuly's is a complex analysis of the play. Summing up this particular line
of argument, she talks of Aristophanes' 'consistent political stance

advocating a liberal extension of citizen rights under the auspices of elite leadership' (2009: 161).

44   Thonemann 2020: 139.

45   Thonemann 2020: 130.

46   Olson 2012: 74.

47   Olson 2012: 78.

Chapter 4

1   The politicians Demostratos and Peisander are mentioned at lines 391 and 490 respectively, and (if the name is not simply appropriated for the sake of a joke) there is a jibe at the expense of a figure called Lysistratos at 1105. There are also mild swipes at a certain Eucrates at line 103 (presumably a naval commander) as well as Euripides at 283.

2   Halliwell 2014: 190. For a brief overview of modern terms relating to humour and laughter, see Robson 2009: 49–53.

3   Halliwell 2014: 189 citing, e.g. Aristotle, *Poetics* 1449a32–7.

4   To be sure, there is a handful of much-discussed lines in tragedy that are potentially 'laugher-inducing', too (e.g. Euripides, *Helen* 435–82; *Ion* 517–62; *Trojan Women* 1050), but these are very much exceptions rather than the norm. See Gregory 2000.

5   For a brief overview and discussion, see Robson 2006: 76–9; Lowe 2008: 7–12 and Swallow 2020: 2–5. A fourth category may be added relating humour to laughter, namely physiological theories.

6   A point made by Lowe 2008: 9, who grapples with the challenge of 'making humour theory work with Aristophanes' in Lowe 2020.

7   There is an untranslatable pun on a place name in the Greek: 'we need to take Pellana'. I have borrowed Sommerstein's 1990 rendering of the pun here: 'thrust up country'.

8   In line 417 there is a pun on *daktulidion*, 'little toe', which the husband unwittingly pronounces as *daktulīdion*, 'little ring', i.e. anus. My attempt to reflect this is a(n admittedly forced) blending of 'tootsie' and 'tush'.

9   Another kind of incongruity of sorts: see Robson 2006: 55–7.

10   A joke possibly underlined in performance by stage business and/or an appropriately disappointed reaction on the part of the women.

11 'Phallic god' is a translation of Konisalos, evidently an (ithy)phallic creature or minor deity associated with Priapus.

12 On the identification of these figures as slaves, see Chapter 2 Section J.

13 Lowe 2008: 26; Silk 1998.

14 For a (masterly and compact) overview of Aristophanes' grammar, see Willi 2003: 232–69.

15 Willi 2003: 244–5 notes that while there are over 600 deictic iotas in Aristophanes, this feature is virtually absent from tragedy, Thucydides and official inscriptions.

16 See Willi 2003: 239.

17 Willi 2003: 241. Aristophanic speakers also favour the dual form (which was slowly being eroded in the spoken language) over the plural: Willi 2002: 123–4.

18 Willi 2003: 174.

19 See Sommerstein1995: 64–8.

20 For definitions of (primary) obscenity, see Henderson 1991a: 2 and Sommerstein 1995: 79. Text-types in which primary obscenities occur outside Old Comedy include iambic poetry, New Comedy, graffiti, curse tablets and magical texts (Bain 1991: 53). For obscenity as a feature of cultic activities, see Henderson, 1991a: 13–17 and O'Higgins 2003, esp. 15–36.

21 On *splekoō*, see Sommerstein 1990: note on line 152 ad loc.; Henderson 1987a: note on line 152 ad loc.; and Henderson 1991a: 154.

22 These lines are composed in (appropriately oracular) dactylic hexameters, with epic flourishes such as the dative plural ending *-essi(n)* (*pterugessin*, 'on wings') and the genitive singular ending *-oio* (*naoio*, 'temple').

23 Sommerstein 1995: 79–80, who just counts four examples, excluding cases where these are uttered in front of an inactive male chorus. Willi 2003: 188 n. 135 lists nine, however, but includes words like *sathē* ('member'?, 'tool'?, *Lysistrata* 1119), which are arguably less jarring than primary obscenities proper.

24 According to the scholiast on this line, which is thus designated Euripides fr. 482 (483 Nauck).

25 On *philia* in *Lysistrata*, see further Robson 2013: 258–61.

26 This is not the case in other Aristophanic plays: the Sausage-Seller claims to 'love' (*phileō*) Demos, at *Knights* 769, for example, and at *Peace* 118 Trygaeus' daughter asks her father 'do you love (*phileis*) me?'.

27   Beale 2010: 61, who compares *Lysistrata*'s presentation of fantastic elements
      to that of Lewis Carroll's *Alice's Adventures in Wonderland*. When Alice first
      hears the White Rabbit speaking, we are told, 'when she thought it over
      afterwards, it occurred to her that she ought to have wondered at this, but at
      the time it all seemed quite natural'.

28   Athens was home to a large number of sex workers, and while the cost of
      sex clearly varied, it could evidently be bought at a low enough price to
      make it widely affordable even to poor Athenians (see Robson 2013: 67–89
      and esp. Loomis 1998: 166–85). Pederastic relationships, typically made up
      of an adult man and an adolescent youth, were more characteristically an
      aristocratic pursuit (for an overview, see Robson 2013: 36–66). It is
      impossible to know, of course, what percentage of Athenian men sought
      extra-marital sexual relations (see Fowler 1996: 248, who suggests: 'most
      men in Aristophanes' audience *did* have sex with their wives and preferred
      it thus').

29   Not that the city is completely devoid of young men before the sex strike. In
      the prologue, Calonice mentions attending to a husband as something that
      might have prevented a woman from arriving at the meeting on time (line 17),
      and one of the old women of the chorus recalls seeing a cavalry officer doing
      his shopping on horseback (561–2). Male slaves (such as the Scythian archers
      who accompany the elderly Proboulos and the attendants who gather outside
      the Acropolis gates in the final scene) do not seem to 'count' in sex-strike terms
      either: they seem neither to be conceived of as viable sexual partners nor to
      suffer its adverse consequences.

30   In these 465 lines, the sex strike is alluded to only briefly at 525–6, 551–4
      and 696–7: see Chapter 2 Section F.

31   A formulation derived from Silk 2000: 224.

32   See Lowe 2006.

33   See Silk 2000: 207–55; the coinage 'recreative' is introduced and explained at
      221.

34   Silk 2000: 207, 209 and 234–5. In *Birds*, for instance, the chorus speak variously
      as birds, chorus members in a play, and as the representatives of the poet
      himself. In *Wasps* and *Frogs*, changes in character are accompanied by changes
      of costume, as the chorus members transform from initiates to frogs and from
      old men to wasps respectively. In his commentary on *Peace*, Sommerstein
      (1985: xviii) notes that the chorus speak with 'four or five distinguishable
      identities' in a space of fewer than 350 lines.

Chapter 5

1 Sommerstein 2009a: 223–36 and 2010. See also Chapter 3 Section A.

2 Revermann 2010: 71.

3 Revermann 2010: 72.

4 Agar 1919.

5 Richards 1912: 223.

6 The view of Sommerstein 2019: 827 is that Rogers' versions of *Lysistrata* and *Thesmophoriazusae* 'hardly deserve the name of translations at all'; tellingly, the English renderings of both plays were published *after* the Greek text in Rogers' editions, rather than on facing pages, which was his normal practice.

7 E.g. Roche 2004. US translators have sometimes given Lampito's speech a Southern States twang. Parker's Lampito is particularly distinctive, uttering such memorable phrases as 'Who-all's notion was this-hyer confabulation?' and 'Hit's right onsettlin' fer gals to sleep all lonely-like withouten no humpin' (Arrowsmith 1969: 14 and 16).

8 Hall 2007: 91 n. 120.

9 Weintraub 1976: 199. For discussion of this 1896 edition and its illustrations, see Walsh 2016b: 231–8.

10 Van Steen 2014a: 756. Donnay had recently enjoyed a modest hit at *le chat noir* with *Phryné* in 1891.

11 The script of Donnay's *Lysistrata* was reworked for further productions of the play in 1896 and 1919; see Beta 2010: 246.

12 For a summary of the play's plot and discussion of its influence, see Van Steen 2000: 110–11, 2014a: 755–6 and 2014b: 441–2, and Beta 2010: 246–7.

13 Van Steen 2016: 759.

14 Van Steen 2000: 78–9. The banning of female spectators and the use of male transvestite actors were also features of the original staging of Demetrakopoulos' plays at the Municipal Theatre.

15 Hall 2007: 86.

16 Quoted by Irvine 2021.

17 It had been published in the UK in 1911, but not copyrighted in the United States and hence was freely available for use. See Tylee 1998: 149 and Hall 2007: 87–8. Interestingly, *Lysistrata* is also the name chosen by the right-wing thinker and writer Anthony Ludovici for an anti-feminist tract published in the UK in 1925.

18 Walton 1987: 341–2.

19 Beta 2010: 250 and 2014: 837. UK theatre owners were presumably keen to see whether *Lysistrata* might repeat the recent success of the play in the United States: see Section D.

20 Van Steen 2000: xiv. Walton 2007: 161 remarks that the far from bowdlerized translation by Fitts 'was treated with leniency' by the censor.

21 Walton 1987: 342.

22 On which see Kotzamani 2005 and Given 2015: 304–9.

23 Kotzamani 2014: 809.

24 Kotzamani 2014: 819–20 also sketches the remarkable influence that this play exercised in the United States for the next thirty years, which witnessed numerous productions based on Seldes' play script and very little interest in the staging of any other Greek comedy.

25 In the Moscow Art Theatre version of the play, for example, Lysistrata is married to Kinesias, and it is she, not Myrrhine, who plays out the temptation scene. The tradition of providing Lysistrata with a husband in adaptations of the play extends back to at least the beginning of the nineteenth century.

26 Kotzamani 2014: 815; Klein 2014: 29.

27 Kotzamani 2014: 817–18, who also discusses the role played by the press in 'discouraging interference' by the censor. See Klein 2014: 23–4 and 31–2 on reactions towards, and the censorship of, this play.

28 Seldes 1934: 5. See also Kotzamani 2014: 818 n. 45; Klein 2014: 31; and Given 2015: 303.

29 Whetmore 2014: 789.

30 See also West 1996; Witham 2003: 72–4; Klein 2014: 43–7 and 57; Whetmore 2014: 787–91.

31 Kotzamani 2014: 819 notes that '[t]here was at least one production of [Seldes' *Lysistrata*] per year throughout the United States in the 1930s and through most of the 1940s and 1950s and into the early 1960s'. These data suggest that a number of post-war productions of *Lysistrata* in the United States are not recorded on the APGRD database: see Section E below.

32 On this film, see Winkler 2014: 907–15 and Klein 2014: 63–86.

33 The debt to *Lysistrata* is acknowledged more than once in the film. Introducing her proposal that the women should not to allow men to 'hug' or 'kiss' them, for example, Liza sings: 'I can give you all the data/ on the girl named Lysistrata,/ so you'll know what a riot she began...'.

34 On musical versions of Aristophanes' plays, see Beta 2010 and 2014 and Given 2015.

35 Klein 2014: 69.
36 See esp. Given 2015: 309–12.
37 See Wrigley 2014: 864–70.
38 *The Times*, January 16, 1964.
39 *The Listener*, January 23, 1954.
40 Quoted by Wrigley 2011, who provides an overview of the production and reactions to it.
41 Maritz 2002: 205.
42 See, e.g., Beta 2010: 255. A particularly notable adaptation in this regard is Robert Fink's opera, *Lysistrata & the War*, written (though ultimately never staged) in the 1960s, see Dutsch 2015: 583.
43 Counting these is not a precise science and the list is not exhaustive; disentangling revivals/repeat performances from new productions is particularly challenging. I have sought to include adaptations of *Lysistrata*, but not productions whose relationship to the original text is categorized 'distant relation'. Database available online: http://www.apgrd.ox.ac.uk/ancient-performance/performances (accessed 31 March 2022).
44 *Hereford Times*, 17 March 2016.
45 Stone on a Walk Theatre website (since updated). Available online: https://web.archive.org/web/20170423055027/http://www.stoneonawalk.com/lysistrata/ (accessed 21 October 2015).
46 Taylor 1993.
47 Alastos 1953: 95; Dickinson 1957: 112; Sommerstein 1973: 184 and 1990: 29; Henderson 1996: 48 and 2000: 285; Halliwell 1997: 100; Kennedy in Slavitt and Bovey 1999: 100; Ruden 2003: 9; Roche 2004: 12; Stuttard 2010: 99; Ewans 2011: 59 and Mulroy 2020: 16. In a similar vein to Dickinson, Fitts 1960: 11 opts for 'sleeping with our men'.
48 Halliwell 2000: 78.
49 Henderson 2002: 508. The version in question, a musical called *Lysistrata: Sex and the City-State* by Gelbart, Menken and Zippel, was substituted for a tamer version of the play penned by the ART's artistic director, Robert Brustein. Brustein is reported as saying that the original musical was 'ferociously obscene – much more than Aristophanes'; so obscene that the leading lady, Cherry Jones, refused to perform it.
50 Halliwell 2002: 124.
51 Zweig 1992.
52 Given 2011: 189.
53 Greer 2011: 5.

54 Robert Butler, writing in the *Independent*, 10 July 1999.

55 Greer 2011: 34.

56 Klein 2014: 87–107.

57 Klein 2014: 93 (quotation); 102.

58 Foley 2012: 68.

59 Seldes 1934: 63.

60 Greer 2011: 46.

61 Harrison 1992: xvi.

62 Harrison 1992: 48.

63 Padley 2008: 4. In the introduction to the UK edition of the play, Harrison 1992: xvi stresses the need for a modern adaptation of *Lysistrata* to play off potent, contemporary tensions: '[i]f I wanted to do *Lysistrata* now I might have to begin again with a third and totally different version'.

64 Severini 2010: 54 documents the background to and origins of the project, noting that, in a telephone interview, 'Blume describe[d] the choice of the play *Lysistrata* itself as accidental'. Yet Blume has also said that '[w]e couldn't have picked a better play if we'd tried' (quoted in Klein 2014: 120).

65 The Lysistrata Project is also the subject of Michael Patrick Kelly's 2008 documentary *Operation Lysistrata*.

66 Severini 2010: 67–8.

67 Hardwick 2010: 83.

68 For further accounts of individual readings, see Kotzamani 2006; Hardwick 2010: 82–4; and Severini 2010: 67–72 and 75–6, who also includes a full list of venues and organizers of readings in an appendix.

69 Kotzamani 2007. The conference was titled 'The Comic Condition as a Play with Incongruities' and held at the University of Tetouan, Morocco (27 April–1 May 2005).

70 Kotzamani 2007: 16, who also includes an interview with Amer about her treatment of *Lysistrata*.

71 El-Ramly 2005. An English extract of the play is available online: http://www.wordswithoutborders.org/article/from-a-peace-of-women (accessed 31 March 2022).

72 Kotzamani 2007: 15. The idea that the peace offered by *Lysistrata* is an untenable fantasy recurs in other stagings, e.g. the Peter Hall production of *Lysistrata* at the Old Vic (1993), the ostensibly celebratory ending of which was interrupted by the lights going out and the sound of machine-gun fire: Goetsch 1993.

73 Borrowing a term from movie-making, Dutsch 2015: 580 and 582 describes this reductive, abstract and ultimately saleable formula as the play's 'high concept'.

74 Weinreich 2008.

75 Blomfield 2011. Note that Weinreich's and Blomfield's press reports were not strictly contemporary with the events in Liberia, but rather appeared in the United States and the UK respectively in 2008, at the time of the release of *Pray the Devil Back to Hell* (a film documenting women's protests during Liberia's civil war); and in 2011, at the time of the joint award of the Nobel Prize to Gbowee.

76 Morales 2013: 295.

77 Morales 2013: 287 and 294 finds the equation between the Liberian situation and *Lysistrata* 'crass and unhelpful', ultimately labelling it as an 'irresponsible use of the classical, in which an ancient text is deployed in a manner that trivializes the modern political debate and silences modern political agents'. See also Dutsch 2015: 585–6.

78 Thus continuing a long, international tradition of *Lysistrata* being adapted in musical form, including opera and operetta: see Beta 2010. A number of critics at the time commented on the opera's accidental topicality in dealing with war: the libretto was written in 1999–2000, long before the allied invasion of Iraq.

79 A character modelled on the real-life figure of Father Michael Pfleger of St. Sabina in Chicago.

80 Jusino 2020 provides a thoughtful account of the ways in which the (perceived) 'hypersexuality' of women relates to, and is ultimately used to undermine, the 'hypermasculinity' of gang culture in the film.

81 Morales 2017.

82 Rosenburg 2015.

83 See for example, Rosenberg 2015 and Dué 2016: 23 and Klein 2020: 62.

84 Klein 2014 and Van Steen 2000.

85 Winkler 2014; Beta 2010, 2014; Given 2015.

86 E.g. Kotzamani 2006 and Klein 2014: 108–26. See also Robson 2016 on the reception of gender and sexuality in Aristophanes, which covers some of the same ground as this chapter.

87 Klein 2014: 103.

Further Reading and Works Cited

Texts, translations and commentaries on *Lysistrata*

Henderson 1987a remains the most comprehensive edition of the Greek text. This edition includes a detailed introduction and copious notes.

Sommerstein's 1990 edition of the play contains a brief introduction, a facing-page translation – which, of all available translations, is perhaps closest to the Greek itself – and plentiful notes. This edition is suitable for the reader with or without Greek.

Henderson's 2000 Loeb Classical Library edition includes the Greek with an often sparky, facing-page translation, plus brief notes and a short introduction.

Henderson's 1996 *Staging Women* volume contains a looser and arguably more performable translation of *Lysistrata*, along with a useful introduction.

Halliwell's 1997 Oxford World Classics translation includes a comprehensive introduction to Aristophanic comedy and represents a sustained attempt to convey the rhythms and linguistic variation of the Greek.

Books on Aristophanes and *Lysistrata*

Useful introductory books on Aristophanes include Dover 1972 and MacDowell 1995, both of which include chapters dedicated to *Lysistrata*. Robson's 2009 book is organized according to topics rather than individual plays, with the chapters 5 and 10 containing the most detailed discussions of *Lysistrata*. Stuttard 2010 is an excellent starting point for anyone new to *Lysistrata*, containing ten short essays on the play. Further helpful introductory pieces include Vaio 1973 and Henderson 1980.

For the reception history of *Lysistrata*, useful starting points are Klein 2014 and many of the chapters in Olson 2014 and Walsh 2016a.

Recommended reading (*) and works cited

Agar, T. L. (1919), 'Obituary Notice of B. B. Rogers', *Classical Review*, 33: 167.

Alastos, D. (1953), *Aristophanes, Two Plays:* Peace *and* Lysistrata. London: Zeno.

Arrowsmith, W. (ed.) (1969), *Aristophanes Four Comedies*: Lysistrata, *The* Acharnians, *The* Congresswomen, *transl. D. Parker, The* Frogs, *transl. R. Lattimore*, Ann Arbor: University of Michigan Press.

Arrowsmith, W. (1973), 'Aristophanes' *Birds*: The Fantasy Politics of Eros', *Arion*, n.s. 1: 119–67.

Austin, and Olson, S. D. (2004), *Aristophanes* Thesmophoriazusae, Oxford: Oxford University Press.

Bain, D. (1991), 'Six Verbs of Sexual Congress', *Classical Quarterly*, 41 (1): 51–77.

Beale, A. (2010), 'Fantasy and Plot in *Lysistrata*', in D. Stuttard (ed.), *Looking at Lysistrata*, 61–9, London: Bristol Classical Press.

Beta, S. (2010), 'The Metamorphosis of a Greek Comedy and Its Protagonist: Some Musical Versions of Aristophanes' *Lysistrata*', in P. Brown and S. Ograjenšek (eds), *Ancient Drama in Music for the Modern Stage*, 240–57, Oxford: Oxford University Press.

Beta, S. (2014), '"Attend, O Muse, Our Holy Dances and Come to Rejoice in Our Songs": The Reception of Aristophanes in the Modern Musical Theater', in S. D. Olson (ed.), *Ancient Comedy and Reception: Essays in Honor of Jeffrey Henderson*, 203–22, Berlin and Boston: De Gruyter.

Blomfield, A. (2011), 'Nobel Peace Prize: Activist Who Used Sex as Weapon for Peace among Three Female Recipients', *The Daily Telegraph*, 7 October.

Bowie, A. M. (1993), *Aristophanes: Myth, Ritual and Comedy*, Cambridge: Cambridge University Press.

Carter, D. M. (2011), 'Plato, Drama, and Rhetoric', in D. M. Carter (ed.), *Why Athens? A Reappraisal of Tragic Politics*, 45–68, Oxford: Oxford University Press.

Colvin, S. (1999), *Dialect in Aristophanes: The Politics of Language in Greek Literature*, Oxford: Clarendon.

Csapo, E. and Goette, H. R. (2007), 'The Men Who Built Theatres: *Theatropolai, Theatronai*, and *Arkhitektones*', in P. Wilson (ed.), *The Greek Theatre and Festivals: Documentary Studies*, 87–121, Oxford and New York: Oxford University Press.

Csapo, E. and Slater, W. J. (1998), *The Context of Ancient Drama*, Ann Arbor: University of Michigan Press.

Dale, A. M. (1956), 'Seen and Unseen on the Greek Stage', *Wiener Studien*, 69: 96–106.

Dawson, S. (1997), 'The Theatrical Audience in Fifth-Century Athens', *Prudentia*, 29: 1–14.

Dickinson, P. (1957), *Aristophanes against War: The* Acharnians, *The* Peace, Lysistrata. London: Oxford University Press.

* Dover, K. J. (1972), *Aristophanic Comedy*, Berkeley and Los Angeles: University of California Press.

Dué, C. (2016), 'Get in Formation, This Is an Emergency: The Politics of Choral Song and Dance in Aristophanes' *Lysistrata* and Spike Lee's *Chi-raq*', *Arion*, 24 (1): 21–54.

Dutsch, D. (2015), 'Democratic Appropriations: *Lysistrata* and Political Activism', in K. Bosher, F. Macintosh, J. McConnell and P. Rankine (eds), *The Oxford Handbook of Greek Drama in the Americas*, 575–94, Oxford: Oxford University Press.

Eidinow, E. (2019), 'Oracles', in A. H. Sommerstein (ed.), *Wiley-Blackwell Encyclopedia of Greek Comedy*, 634–6, Wiley-Blackwell: Hoboken.

El-Ramly, L. (2005), *Salam El-Nisaa*. Cairo: Masr El-Mahrousa Publishing House.

Ewans, M. C. (2011), *Aristophanes*: Lysistrata, The Women's Festival, *and* Frogs, Norman: University of Oklahoma Press.

* Faraone, C. A. (1997), 'Salvation and Female Heroics in the Parodos of Aristophanes' *Lysistrata*', *Journal of Hellenic Studies*, 117: 38–59.

Faraone, C. A. (2006), 'Priestess and Courtesan: The Ambivalence of Female Leadership in Aristophanes' *Lysistrata*', in C. A. Faraone and L. K. McClure, *Prostitutes and Courtesans in the Ancient World*, Wisconsin: University of Wisconsin Press.

Fitts, D. (1960), *Aristophanes* Lysistrata, London: Faber and Faber.

* Fletcher, J. (1999), 'Sacrificial Bodies and the Body of the Text in Aristophanes' *Lysistrata*', *Ramus*, 28 (2): 108–25.

Foley, H. P. (2012), *Reimagining Greek Tragedy on the American Stage*, Berkeley, Los Angeles and London: University of California Press.

Fowler, R. L. (1996), 'How the *Lysistrata* Works', *Echos du Monde Classique/Classical Views*, 15 (2): 245–9.

Gilhuly, K. (2009), *The Feminine Matrix of Sex and Gender in Classical Athens*, Cambridge: Cambridge University Press.

Given, J. (2011), 'Staging the Reconciliation Scene of Aristophanes' *Lysistrata*', *Didaskalia*, 8: 189–97.

Given, J. (2015), 'Aristophanic Comedy in American Musical Theatre, 1925–1969', in K. Bosher, F. Macintosh, J. McConnell and P. Rankine (eds), *The Oxford Handbook of Greek Drama in the Americas*, 575–94, Oxford: Oxford University Press.

Goetsch, S. (1993), 'Reviews: Aristophanes' *Lysistrata*, The Old Vic', *Electronic Antiquity* 1 (3). Available online: scholar.lib.vt.edu/ejournals/ElAnt/V1N3/goetsch.html (accessed 31 March 2022).

Goldhill, S. D. (1994), 'Representing Democracy: Women at the Great Dionysia', in R. G. Osborne and S. Hornblower (eds), *Ritual, Finance, Politics: Athenian Democratic Accounts Presented to David Lewis*, 347–70, Oxford: Oxford University Press.

Greer, G. (2011), *Lysistrata – The Sex Strike, after Aristophanes*, adapted for performance with additional material by P. Willmott, London: Samuel French.

Gregory, J. (2000), 'Comic Elements in Euripides', in M. J. Cropp, K. H. Lee, and D. Sansone (eds), *Euripides and Tragic Theatre in the Late Fifth Century*, 59–74, Champaign: Stipes.

Habash, M. (2019), '"Lenaean Theatre"', in A. H. Sommerstein (ed.), *Wiley-Blackwell Encyclopedia of Greek Comedy*, 493–4, Wiley-Blackwell: Hoboken.

Hall, E. (2007), 'The English-Speaking Aristophanes 1650–1914', in E. Hall and F. Macintosh, *Greek Tragedy and the British Theatre 1660–1914*, 66–92, Oxford: Oxford University Press.

* Hall, E. (2010), 'The Many Faces of Lysistrata', in D. Stuttard (ed.), *Looking at Lysistrata*, 29–36, London: Bristol Classical Press.

Halliwell, S. (1980), 'Aristophanes' Apprenticeship', *Classical Quarterly* 30 (1): 33–45.

* Halliwell, S. (1997), *Aristophanes* Birds *and Other Plays*, Oxford: Oxford University Press.

Halliwell, S. (2000), 'Aristophanes' in O. Chase (ed.), *Encyclopedia of Literary Translation into English*, 77–8, London and Chicago: Fitzroy Dearborn Press.

Halliwell, S. (2002), 'Aristophanic Sex: The Erotics of Shamelessness', in M. C. Nussbaum and J. Sihvola (eds), *The Sleep of Reason: Erotic Experience and Social Ethics in Ancient Greece and Rome*, 120–42, Chicago and London: University of Chicago Press.

Halliwell, S. (2014), 'Laughter', in M. Revermann (ed.), *Cambridge Companion to Greek Comedy*, 189–205, Cambridge: Cambridge University Press.

Hardwick, L. (2010), '*Lysistrata*s on the Modern Stage', in D. Stuttard, *Looking at Lysistrata*, 80–90, London: Bristol Classical Press.

Harrison, T. (1992), *The Common Chorus: A Version of Aristophanes'* Lysistrata, London: Faber and Faber.

Hartwig, A. (2019), 'Competitors, Number of', in A. H. Sommerstein (ed.), *Wiley-Blackwell Encyclopedia of Greek Comedy*, 215–16, Wiley-Blackwell: Hoboken.

Harvey, F. D. (1994), 'Lacomica: Aristophanes and the Spartans', in A. Powell and S. Hodkinson (eds), *The Shadow of Sparta*, 35–58, London and New York: Routledge.

Hawkins, T. (2001), 'Seducing a Misanthrope: Timon the Philogynist in Aristophanes' *Lysistrata*', *Greek, Roman and Byzantine Studies*, 42 (2): 143–62.

* Henderson, J. (1980), '*Lysistrate*: The Play and its Themes', *Yale Classical Studies*, 26: 153–218.

* Henderson, J. (1987a), *Aristophanes* Lysistrata, Oxford: Clarendon.

* Henderson, J. (1987b), 'Older Women in Attic Comedy', *Transactions of the American Philological Association*, 117: 105–29.

Henderson, J. (1991a), *The Maculate Muse: Obscene Language in Attic Comedy*, 2nd edn, New York and Oxford: Oxford University Press.

Henderson, J. (1991b). 'Women and the Athenian Dramatic Festivals', *Transactions of the American Philological Association*, 121: 133–47.

* Henderson, J. (1996), *Three Plays by Aristophanes: Staging Women*, New York and London: Routledge.

* Henderson, J. (2000), *Aristophanes*: Birds, Lysistrata, Women at the Thesmophoria, Loeb Classical Library, Cambridge, Massachusetts: Harvard University Press.

Henderson, J. (2002), 'Epilogue', *American Journal of Philology*, 123: 501–11.

Henderson, J. (2019), 'Women in Audience', in A. H. Sommerstein (ed.), *Wiley-Blackwell Encyclopedia of Greek Comedy*, 1018–19, Wiley-Blackwell: Hoboken.

Irvine, A. D. (2021), 'Aristophanes' *Lysistrata*: A Fair and Honest Peace', *Antigone*. Available online: https://antigonejournal.com/2021/04/aristophanes-lysistrata/ (accessed 31 March 2022).

Jusino, E. (2020), 'Riffing on *Lysistrata*: Gender and Social Critique in Spike Lee's *Chi-raq*', *Museion*, 17 (1): 51–68.

* Klein, E. (2014), *Sex and War on the American Stage*: Lysistrata *in Performance 1930–2012*, New York and London: Routledge.

Klein, E. (2020), 'Seductive Movements in *Lysistrata* and Spike Lee's *Chi-raq*: Activism, Adaptation and Immersive Theatre in Film', *Adaptation*, 13 (1): 59–76.

Korres, M. (2002), 'Modell des Dionysos-Theaters', in *Die griechische Klassik – Idee oder Wirklichkeit?*, Antikensammlungen Berlin, Staatliche Museen Preußischer Kulturbesitz (exhibition catalogue), 540–1, Mainz: Musée.

Kotzamani, M. (2005), '*Lysistrata* Joins the Soviet Revolution: Aristophanes as Engaged Theatre', in J. Dillon and S. E. Wilmer (eds), *Rebel Women: Staging Ancient Greek Drama Today*, 78–111, Methuen: London.

Kotzamani, M. (2006), 'Artist Citizens in the Age of the Web: The Lysistrata Project (2003–present)', *Theater*, 36: 103–10.

Kotzamani, M. (2007), '*Lysistrata* on Arabic Stages', *Performing Arts Journal*, 83: 13–41.

Kotzamani, M. (2014), '*Lysistrata* on Broadway', in S. D. Olson (ed.), *Ancient Comedy and Reception: Essays in Honor of Jeffrey Henderson*, 807–23, Berlin and Boston: De Gruyter.

Lambert, M. (2018), 'Mapping Women's Bodies and the Male "Gaze": Reconciliation in Aristophanes' *Lysistrata*', *Akroterion*, 63: 35–56.

le Guen, B. (2019), 'Lenaea', in A. H. Sommerstein (ed.), *Wiley-Blackwell Encyclopedia of Greek Comedy*, 492–3, Wiley-Blackwell: Hoboken.

Lear, A. and Cantarella, E. (2008), *Images of Ancient Pederasty: Boys Were Their Gods*, Routledge: London and New York.

Lewis, D. M. (1955), 'Notes on Attic Inscriptions (II): XXIII. Who was Lysistrata?', *Annual of the British School at Athens*, 50: 1–36.

Loomis, W. (1998), *Wages, Welfare Costs and Inflation in Classical Athens*, Ann Arbor: University of Michigan Press.

Lowe, N. J. (2006), 'Aristophanic Spacecraft', in L. Kozak and J. Rich (eds), *Playing Around Aristophanes*, 48–64, Warminster: Aris & Phillips.

* Lowe, N. J. (2008), *Comedy: Greece & Rome, New Surveys in the Classics 37*, Cambridge: Cambridge University Press.

Lowe, N. J. (2020), 'Beyond a Joke: Making Humour Theory Work with Aristophanes', in P. Swallow and E. Hall (eds), *Aristophanic Humour: Theory and Practice*, 13–22, London: Bloomsbury Academic.

MacDowell, D. M. (1994), 'The Number of Speaking Actors in Old Comedy', *Classical Quarterly*, 44 (2): 325–35.

* MacDowell, D. M. (1995), *Aristophanes and Athens: An Introduction to the Plays*, Oxford: Oxford University Press.

Maritz, J. (2002), 'Greek Drama in Rhodesia/Zimbabwe', in J. Barsby (ed.), *Greek and Roman Drama: Translation and Performance*, 197–215, Stuttgart and Weimar: Metzler.

Marshall, C. W. (2014), 'Dramatic Technique and Athenian Comedy', in
M. Revermann (ed.), *Cambridge Companion to Greek Comedy*, 131–46,
Cambridge: Cambridge University Press.

* McClure, L. M. (2015), 'Courtesans Reconsidered: Women in Aristophanes'
Lysistrata', *EuGeStA*, 5: 54–84.

* Morales, H. (2013), 'Aristophanes' *Lysistrata*, the Liberian "Sex Strike", and the
Politics of Reception', *Greece & Rome*, 60: 281–95.

Morales, H. (2017), '(Sex) Striking Out: Spike Lee's *Chi-raq*', *Eidolon*. Available
online: https://eidolon.pub/sex-striking-out-spike-lee-s-chi-raq-f18fe17
dd86b (accessed 31 March 2022).

Muecke, F. (1998), 'Oracles in Aristophanes', *Seminari Romani di Cultura Greca*,
1: 257–74.

Mulroy, D. (2020), Lysistrata: *A New Verse Translation*, Madison: University of
Wisconsin Press.

O'Higgins, L. (2003), *Women and Humor in Classical Greece*, Cambridge:
Cambridge University Press.

Olson, S. D. (2002), *Aristophanes* Acharnians, Oxford: Oxford University Press.

Olson, S. D. (2010), 'Comedy, Politics, and Society', in G. W. Dobrov (ed.), *Brill's
Companion to the Study of Greek Comedy*, Leiden and Boston: Brill.

* Olson, S. D. (2012), '*Lysistrata*'s Conspiracy and the Politics of 412 BC', in
C. W. Marshall and G. Kovacs (eds), *No Laughing Matter: Studies in Athenian
Comedy*, 68–81, London: Bristol Classical Press.

* Olson, S. D. (ed.) (2014), *Ancient Comedy and Reception: Essays in Honor of
Jeffrey Henderson*, Berlin and Boston: De Gruyter.

Padley, S. (2008), '"Hijacking Culture": Tony Harrison and the Greeks', *Cycnos*, 18
(1). Available online: https://epi-revel.univ-cotedazur.fr/publication/item/328
(accessed 31 March 2022).

Parker, L. P. E. (1997), *The Songs of Aristophanes*, Oxford: Clarendon.

Prince, C. K. (2009), 'The Lioness & The Cheesegrater (Ar. *Lys.* 231–32)', *Studi
Italiani di Filologia Classica* 7 (2): 149–75.

Revermann, M. (2006), *Comic Business: Theatricality, Dramatic Technique, and
Performance Contexts of Aristophanic Comedy*, Oxford and New York: Oxford
University Press.

* Revermann, M. (2010), 'On Misunderstanding the *Lysistrata*, Productively', in
D. Stuttard, *Looking at Lysistrata*, 70–9, London: Bristol Classical Press.

Richards, H. (1912), 'The Lysistrata of Aristophanes', *Classical Review*, 26 (7):
223–4.

Robson, J. (2006), *Humour, Obscenity and Aristophanes*, Tübingen: Narr.

* Robson, J. (2009), *Aristophanes: An Introduction*, London: Duckworth.

Robson, J. (2013), *Sex and Sexuality in Classical Athens*, Edinburgh: Edinburgh University Press.

Robson, J. (2015), 'Fantastic Sex: Fantasies of Sexual Assault in Aristophanes', in M. Masterson, N. S. Rabinowitz and J. Robson (eds), *Sex in Antiquity: Reconsidering Gender and Sexuality in the Ancient World*, 315–31, Abingdon and New York: Routledge.

Robson, J. (2016), 'Aristophanes, Gender and Sexuality', in P. Walsh (ed.), *Brill's Companion to the Reception of Aristophanes*, 44–66: Leiden and Boston.

Robson, J. (2017), 'Humouring the Masses: The Theatre Audience and the Highs and Lows of Aristophanic Comedy', in L. Grig (ed.), *Popular Culture in the Ancient World*, 66–87, Cambridge: Cambridge University Press.

Roche, P. (2004), *Four Plays by Aristophanes*, Signet Classics: New York and London.

Roselli, D. K. (2011), *Theater of the People: Spectators and Society in Ancient Athens*, Austin: University of Texas Press.

Rosen, R. (2018), 'Sparta and Spartans in Old Comedy', in P. Cartledge and A. Powell (eds), *The Greek Superpower: Sparta in the Self-Definitions of Athenians*, 139–55, Swansea: The Classical Press of Wales.

Rosenburg, A. (2015), '*Chi-raq* and Spike Lee's Political Vision', *Washington Post*, 4 December.

Ruden, S. (2003), *Aristophanes* Lysistrata, Indianapolis: Hackett.

Russo, C. F. (1994), *Aristophanes: An Author for the Stage*, London and New York: Routledge.

Rutherford, R. B. (2015), '*Lysistrata* and Female Song', *Classical Quarterly*, 65 (2): 60–8.

Scullion, S. (1994), *Three Studies in Athenian Dramaturgy*, Stuttgart and Leipzig: Teubner.

Seldes, G. (1934), Lysistrata *by Aristophanes: A New Version by Gilbert Seldes with a Special Introduction by Mr. Seldes and Illustrations by Pablo Picasso*, New York: Limited Editions Club.

Severini, G. C. (2010), 'From Elite to Inclusive: *Lysistrata* and Gender, Democracy, and War', MA diss., University of Alberta.

Silk, M. S (1998), 'Putting on a Dionysus Show', *Times Literary Supplement*, 28 August.

Silk, M. S. (2000), *Aristophanes and the Definition of Comedy*, Oxford: Oxford University Press.

Slavitt, D. R. and Bovie, P. (eds) (1999), *Aristophanes, 2*, Philadelphia: University of Pennsylvania Press.

Smith, N. D. (2017), 'Aristophanes' "Lysistrata" and the Two Acropolis Priestesses', *The International Journal of Literary Humanities*, 15 (3): 35–40.

Sommerstein, A. H. (1973), *The* Acharnians, *The* Clouds, Lysistrata, Penguin: Harmondsworth.

Sommerstein A. H. (1977), 'Aristophanes and the Events of 411', *Journal of Hellenic Studies*, 97: 112–26.

Sommerstein, A. H. (1985), *The Comedies of Aristophanes, Vol. 5*: Peace, Warminster: Aris & Phillips.

* Sommerstein, A. H. (1990), *The Comedies of Aristophanes, Vol. 7*: Lysistrata, Warminster: Aris & Phillips.

* Sommerstein, A. H. (1995), 'The Language of Athenian Women', in F. De Martino and A. H. Sommerstein (eds), *Lo Spettacolo delle Voci*, Part 2, 61–85, Bari: Levante.

Sommerstein, A. H. (1996), 'How to Avoid Being a *Komodoumenos*', *Classical Quarterly*, 46 (2): 327–56.

Sommerstein, A. H. (1997), 'The Theatre Audience, The *dēmos* and the *Suppliants* of Aeschylus', in C. Pelling (ed.), *Greek Tragedy and the Historian*, 63–79, Oxford: Clarendon.

* Sommerstein, A. H. (2009a), 'Lysistrata the Warrior', in A. H. Sommerstein (ed.), *Talking about Laughter*, 223–36, Oxford: Oxford University Press.

Sommerstein, A. H. (2009b), 'Nudity, Obscenity and Power: Modes of Female Assertiveness in Aristophanes', in A. H. Sommerstein (ed.), *Talking about Laughter*, 237–53, Oxford: Oxford University Press.

Sommerstein, A. H. (2010), 'Lysistrata the Warrior', in D. Stuttard (ed.), *Looking at Lysistrata*, 37–48, London: Bristol Classical Press.

Sommerstein, A. H. (2017), 'How "Popular" was Athenian Comedy?' *Quaderni Urbinati di Cultura Classica*, n.s. 116 (2): 11–26.

Sommerstein, A. H. (2019), 'Rogers, Benjamin Bickley' in A. H. Sommerstein (ed.), *Wiley-Blackwell Encyclopedia of Greek Comedy*, 827, Wiley-Blackwell: Hoboken.

Storey, I. C. (2019), *Aristophanes*: Peace, London: Bloomsbury Academic.

Storey, I. C. and Allan, A. (2005), *A Guide to Ancient Greek Drama*, Blackwell: Malden, Oxford and Carlton.

Stroup, S. C. (2004), 'Designing Women: Aristophanes' *Lysistrata* and the "Hetairization" of the Greek Wife', *Arethusa*, 37 (1): 37–73.

* Stuttard, D. (ed.) (2010), *Looking at Lysistrata*, London: Bristol Classical Press.

Swallow, P. (2020), 'Dissecting the Frog(s)', in P. Swallow and E. Hall (eds), *Aristophanic Humour: Theory and Practice*, 1–9, London: Bloomsbury Academic.

Taplin, O. (1978), *Greek Tragedy in Action*, Routledge: London and New York.

Taylor, P. (1993), 'All Present and Erect', *The Independent*, 16 June.

Thonemann, P. (2020), 'Lysimache and *Lysistrata*', *Journal of Hellenic Studies*, 140: 128–40.

Tsoumpra, N. (2020), 'More Than Just a Sex-Strike: A Case of Medical Pathology in *Lysistrata*', *Classical Journal*, 116 (1): 1–20.

Tylee, C. M. (1998), '"A Better World for Both": Men, Cultural Transformation and the Suffragettes', in M. Joannou and J. Purvis (eds), *The Women's Suffrage Movement: New Feminist Perspectives*, 140–56, Manchester and New York: Manchester University Press.

* Vaio, J. (1973), 'The Manipulation of Theme and Action in Aristophanes' *Lysistrata*', *Greek, Roman and Byzantine Studies*, 14 (4): 369–80.

* Van Steen, G. (2000), *Venom in Verse: Aristophanes in Modern Greece*, Princeton: Princeton University Press.

Van Steen, G. (2014a), 'Close Encounters of the Comic Kind: Aristophanes' *Frogs* and *Lysistrata* in Athenian Mythological Burlesques of the 1880s', in S. D. Olson (ed.), *Ancient Comedy and Reception: Essays in Honor of Jeffrey Henderson*, 747–61, Berlin and Boston: De Gruyter.

Van Steen, G. (2014b), 'Snapshots of Aristophanes and Menander: From Spontaneous Reception to Belated Reception Study', in M. Revermann (ed.), *The Cambridge Companion to Greek Comedy*, 433–50, Cambridge: Cambridge University Press.

Van Steen, G. (2016), 'Comedy and Tragedy in Agon(y): The 1902 Comedy *Panathenaia* of Andreas Nikolaras', in P. Walsh (ed.), *Brill's Companion to the Reception of Aristophanes*, 240–62, Brill: Leiden and Boston.

Von Wilamowitz-Moellendorff, U. (1927), *Aristophanes* Lysistrate, Berlin: Weidmann.

* Walsh, P. (ed.) (2016a), *Brill's Companion to the Reception of Aristophanes*, Brill: Leiden and Boston.

Walsh, P. (2016b), 'The Verbal and the Visual: Aristophanes' Nineteenth-Century English Translators' in P. Walsh (ed.), *Brill's Companion to the Reception of Aristophanes*, 217–39, Brill: Leiden and Boston.

Walton, J. M. (1987), 'Revival: England', in J. M. Walton (ed.), *Living Greek Theatre: A Handbook of Classical Performance and Modern Production*, 329–54, Westport, CT: Greenwood Press.

Walton, J. M. (2007), 'Good Manners, Decorum and the Public Peace: Greek Drama and the Censor', in F. Billiani (ed.), *Modes of Censorship and Translation: National Contexts and Diverse Media*, 143–66, Routledge: London and New York.

Weinreich, R. (2008), 'Pray the Devil Back to Hell', *Gossip Central*, 11 November.

Weintraub, S. (1976), *Aubrey Beardsley: Imp of the Perverse*, University Park: Penn State University Press.

West, R. (1996), 'Others, Adults, Censored: The Federal Theatre Project's Black *Lysistrata* Cancellation', *Theatre Survey*, 37 (2), 93–113.

Whetmore, K. J. (2014), 'She (Don't) Gotta Have It: African-American Reception of *Lysistrata*', in S. D. Olson (ed.), *Ancient Comedy and Reception: Essays in Honor of Jeffrey Henderson*, 786–96, Berlin and Boston: De Gruyter.

Wiles, D. (1997), *Tragedy in Athens: Performance Space and Theatrical Meaning*, Cambridge: Cambridge University Press.

Wiles, D. (2000), *Greek Theatre Performance: An Introduction*, Cambridge: Cambridge University Press.

Willi, A. (2002), 'Languages on Stage: Aristophanic Language, Cultural History, and Athenian Identity', in A. Willi (ed.), *The Language of Greek Comedy*, 111–49, Oxford: Oxford University Press.

Willi, A. (2003), T*he Languages of Aristophanes: Aspects of Linguistic Variation in Classical Attic Greek*, Oxford: Oxford University Press.

Wilson, N. G. (2007), *Aristophanis Fabulae. Tomus II.* Lysistrata, Thesmophoriazusae, Ranae, Ecclesiazusae, *Plutus*, Oxford: Oxford University Press.

Wilson, P. (2000), *The Athenian Institution of the* Khoregia: *The Chorus, the City, the Stage*, Cambridge: Cambridge University Press.

Winkler, M. M. (2014), 'Aristophanes in the Cinema; or, the Metamorphoses of *Lysistrata*', in S. D. Olson (ed.), *Ancient Comedy and Reception: Essays in Honor of Jeffrey Henderson*, 894–944, Berlin and Boston: De Gruyter.

Witham, B. (2003), *The Federal Theatre Project: A Case Study*, Cambridge: Cambridge University Press.

Wrigley, A. (2011), 'Greek Plays: *Lysistrata* (BBC, 1964)', *Screen Plays: Theatre Plays on British Television*, 28 June. Available online: https://screenplaystv. wordpress.com/2011/06/28/lysistrata-bbc-1964/ (accessed 31 March 2022).

Wrigley, A. (2014), 'Aristophanes at the BBC, 1940s–1960s', in S. D. Olson (ed.), *Ancient Comedy and Reception: Essays in Honor of Jeffrey Henderson*, 849–70, Berlin and Boston: De Gruyter.

Zweig, B. (1992), 'The Mute Nude Female Characters in Aristophanes' Plays', in A. Richlin (ed.), *Pornography and Representation in Greece and Rome*, 73–89, New York and Oxford: Oxford University Press.

Index